TASTES *of the* PACIFIC NORTHWEST

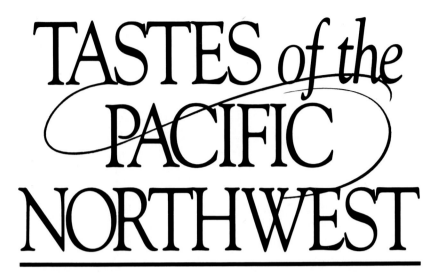

TASTES *of the* PACIFIC NORTHWEST

Traditional & Innovative Recipes from America's Newest Regional Cuisine

•

BY FRED BRACK & TINA BELL

Foreword by Judith Olney

Design by Elizabeth Watson

From the Editors of
Washington Magazine

Doubleday

New York

Published by Doubleday, a division of Bantam Doubleday
Dell Publishing Group, Inc., 666 Fifth Avenue, New York,
New York 10103.

"Doubleday" and the portrayal of an anchor with a dolphin
are trademarks of Doubleday, a division of Bantam Doubleday Dell Publishing Group, Inc.

Published by arrangement with
The Evergreen Publishing Company, Seattle

Address correspondence to:
David W. Fuller, Managing Editor
Evergreen Publishing Company
901 Lenora, Seattle, WA 98121

Library of Congress 88-3537
Library of Congress Cataloging in Publication Data Applied For
ISBN 0-385-24387-1

TABLE OF CONTENTS

FOREWORD

Sometimes my profession dictates that I climb onto planes and travel from city to city for weeks at a stretch. Now, this is not a life I'd choose to lead full time. But it does allow for an extraordinary national overview and an objectivity that arises when one substitutes one's banal, earthbound existence for an airborne one. If in mundane life the skies beckon and intrigue, so in turn does life in the sky soon grow tedious. Then the earth excites again, and one drops out of the air to skin the cream off the top of brief destinations. Thus, people who tend to travel a lot develop a kind of shorthand characterization of towns and regions, and address books full of tasty nuggets of information.

What the traveler often gets are cursory, homogenized views of buildings topped with bleak plastic logos and signs advertising only vistas of the known. What regionality should provide is spice and diversity, strange freckles and warts of ethnocentricity. We scan faces and figures for clues to the local ethos. We go to places, after all, for doses of something other than what we are—change, new scenery, differing styles of art and architecture, strange tastes, jolting sensations.

If you are, like I am, a lover of food, it is the tastes that linger in the mind. The odd characterizing foodstuffs for which I search draw me back to a place and seem to be one with the people and their aura, giving a region its peculiar face. It is pine-nut candies, terra-cotta-colored chili pepper bread and blue corn chips that spring from the Indian-blanket hues of the gritty desert Southwest. It is the rotund roués and sassy spices, the beignets plump as denizens of a bordello that conjure New Orleans. And it is sturgeon and salmon with ice-water-crisp flesh, and fruit the colors of plaid logger's shirts, fruit as large as Eden's, fruit flourishing in the clean pine air, that revive my memories of the Pacific Northwest. (How many of us have gotten our first taste of Northwest abundance when those magic boxes of swaddled fruit arrived in the holidays of our childhood, and our parents gave us the one lush pear wrapped in gilt foil? Nectar dribbled from those perfumed fruits, and golden rings and necklaces were fashioned from those foils.)

The remarkable thing is that even as little as 10 years ago, regionality was best explored on continents other than our own. It was easy to go to France and immediately understand how Provence gave rise to a limited socio-cuisine. The salt and lavender-scented air, the gnarled olive trees and the very weeds of the earth (thyme, oregano, rosemary) have dictated the food for centuries, so that bourrides and bouillabaisses stand perfected by time and repetition, full-blown intrinsic beings. The dishes almost have palpable souls. They breathe out through the very pores of the Provencaux who ingest them, and you sniff faint bouillabaisse on any laden bus in Marseilles.

On our continent, the evocation of regionality was a newer obsession. I remember attending a seminar a few years back on "California Cuisine," at which several food luminaries floundered in attempts to define their topic, which was not so strange when one stopped to think that the entire cuisine had only just been christened. What was exciting was the pioneering spirit of passionate, venturesome young cooks who demanded extraordinary produce, and dedicated producers who filled those demands, all of whom would in time, I think, polish and perfect the bouillabaisse of California's future (and it may be the issue of some Occidental/Oriental marriage). What makes the struggle to define a regional cuisine most precious and such a happy, embracing venture is that cooks in so many regions are still staking out and perfecting the ingredients that are "theirs," and that they will in time export to the rest of us. They are still experimenting and refining those ingredients into thoughtful culinary compositions and sharing them.

Such a sharing is evident in this bright book by Fred Brack and Tina Bell. Their love for, and knowledge of, the region is abundantly evident, and I like their frank bafflement about "Northwest Cuisine." "We don't," they say, "know what that is." That admitted, they ply us with Dungeness Crab Ravioli with Lemon-Caper Butter and Farmhouse Potato Custard Pie, Walla Walla Sweet Onion Tart and Pears on Pastry with Oregon Blue Cheese and Blueberry Coulis. Most remarkable is their Salmon Hash. The psychology of the dish is simply brilliant. That regal, kingly fish is humbled to a lowly lumberjack's hash; that common diner food is pitched to a rich man's heights. Therein lies a whole literature of food, and on such a cornerstone, at least, will a regional cuisine soon build its solid edifice. I like this book, its spirit and its recipes very much, and I think you will too.

Judith Olney

INTRODUCTION

Fresh! professional chefs cried out. Fresh, their customers agreed. Fresh, home cooks echoed in their kitchens.

And thus a revolution occurred in North American cooking.

Fresh! meant more than not-frozen or not-canned. It meant fruits and vegetables, fish and shellfish, herbs and even meats and poultry that came to the kitchen in the full bloom of their flavors and aromas. To meet the demand, distribution lines from producer to cook often shortened. Some cooks actually became acquainted with the people who grow and harvest their food, a return to a simpler time.

"Regional cooking" became the catchword for culinary excitement, as chefs and cooks turned their attention to ingredients in their own backyards.

That's when the Pacific Northwest proudly stepped forward. Well, actually it took a while. Our region, last to be settled during the march west, exists not only on the edge of the continent but also on the periphery of public consciousness. Finally, however, people elsewhere are learning that the Pacific Northwest is extraordinarily endowed with good things to eat.

For this we owe gratitude to sea and soil, to mountains that catch moist winds from the Pacific Ocean and divide the region into wet and dry sides, and to long summer days and cool nights.

We can, and do, grow nearly everything grown elsewhere on the continent except citrus. (Remarkably, one fellow in British Columbia's Okanagan Valley, with the help of a greenhouse, even does that. Bananas, too!) For some crops, we're the continent's principal supplier. Apples. Blackberries. Raspberries. Asparagus. Mint. Hops. Dried peas and lentils. Pears. Big baking potatoes. Sweet cherries.

From the ocean and many inland waters and rivers flowing powerfully to the sea we harvest a remarkable array of fish and shellfish. Salmon, of course. And oysters. But also sturgeon, cod, sole, mussels, shrimp, scallops, halibut, dozens of varieties of rockfish and, from the farming ponds of Idaho, rainbow trout.

Rangeland on the dry side of the mountains feeds beef cattle. River valleys shelter cows and goats, from whose milk come distinctive cheeses.

And, in little more than a decade, newly planted vineyards have begun pouring forth premium wines that are catching the world's attention.

These are our blessings, and the purpose of this book is to celebrate them and to acquaint those who might not fully appreciate the Pacific Northwest's bounty with the region's culinary wonders.

The recipes offered come from several sources. Some Tina Bell developed for her Seattle delicatessen, The Wedge. Others were devised for the book. And others were generously supplied by cooks, professional and amateur, who take pride in their region's provender.

Finally, a word about "Northwest Cuisine." We don't know what that is. In fact, we doubt that such a thing exists, though some overly zealous boosters have attempted to package the ideas and discoveries of the region's venturesome cooks under that label. What these cooks share, however, is not a settled, codified approach to the kitchen but an appreciation of Pacific Northwest ingredients and the virtues of Fresh!

Our hope is that you will, too.

Fred Brack and Tina Bell
Seattle, Washington, 1988

NOTES ON INGREDIENTS

Balsamic vinegar: This mellow red vinegar from Italy is widely available in specialty food stores. Several recipes in *The Tastes of the Pacific Northwest* call for it. If it's not available, red wine vinegar may be substituted, although the taste will not be the same since balsamic is not fermented and therefore is not sour.

Butter: Although butter once was salted to preserve it, nowadays it's salted because people have grown accustomed to the taste. Salted and unsalted butter may be used interchangeably in the recipes presented here, although all were developed and tested with unsalted butter. In those recipes that we think must have unsalted butter, we have specified it.

Court boullion: For poaching fish, this is the classic liquid:

> To 4 quarts water, add 1 chopped onion, 1 chopped carrot, 1 chopped celery stalk with leaves, 2 sprigs parsley and 1 tablespoon salt. Boil 15 minutes, add 2 cups dry white wine and simmer 10 minutes.

Crème fraîche: Here are two easy methods of preparing this thick, lightly cultured cream. (Unpasteurized cream is best.)

> Mix 1 tablespoon buttermilk into 1 cup heavy cream. Cover and let stand at room temperature 12-24 hours, until thick. Cream may be refrigerated after that for several days and will thicken further.

Or:

> Whip 1 cup sour cream to incorporate air. Heat 1 1/2 cups heavy cream until lukewarm. Remove from heat and stir in sour cream. Cover and let stand at room temperature overnight, until thick. Cream may be refrigerated after that for several days and will thicken further.

Hazelnuts: Toasting greatly enhances the flavor of hazelnuts. Spread nuts in shallow pan and cook at 275° F for 20-30 minutes. Rub nuts in a towel or rough cloth to remove skins.

Herbs: Fresh herbs are better, by far. When substituting dried for fresh, use half as much.

Parsley: Flat-leaf, "Italian" parsley has more flavor and is therefore more desirable than its cousin.

Pepper: Ground pepper quickly loses flavor. If possible, always use freshly ground.

Red peppers: To roast sweet peppers, try this easy method: quarter peppers, seed and cut out cores. Place skin side up on a baking sheet and place under broiler as close as possible. When skins blacken, place peppers in paper bag for 15-20 minutes. Peel off skins.

Scallion: This is the term we've used for the vegetable also called "green onion."

Stock: Whether vegetable, meat or fish, high-quality stocks are essential to the final flavor of many dishes in this book. The home cook, however, often hasn't the time to prepare them. In the case of chicken, canned stock isn't too bad, especially if it's boiled down by about a third to concentrate flavor. In the case of beef, we suggest freshening canned stock using the following method devised by the late Michael Field, a food writer and cooking teacher:

> Quarter 2 small onions (or 1 large). Brown the onions in 2 tablespoons butter. Add 3/4 cup white wine to the pan and boil to reduce to 1/2 cup. Add 4 cups canned beef stock or bouillon, a chopped carrot, 2 peeled cloves of garlic, 1/2 teaspoon thyme, a bay leaf, some parsley and/or celery tops and, if available, the white part of a leek, chopped. Half-cover the pan and simmer 30-45 minutes. Strain before using.

If you have time, canned chicken stock can

be freshened in this way:

To 4 cups canned chicken stock, add 1 chopped onion, 1 chopped carrot, 1/2 chopped celery stalk, 1/2 bay leaf, 1/4 teaspoon thyme, some parsley and, if available, the white part of a leek, chopped. Half-cover the pan and simmer 30-45 minutes. Strain before using.

For fish stock, canned or bottled clam juice often can serve as an adequate substitute. However, fish stock is relatively easy to prepare. Any standard recipe will do. Here's one method:

To 5-7 cups water add 1 medium chopped onion, 2 small chopped carrots, 1 stalk chopped celery, 6-8 white peppercorns, 1 bay leaf, 2-3 sprigs parsley, 1 teaspoon fresh thyme (or 1/2 teaspoon dried), 2 cups dry white wine and 2-3 pounds fish bones, heads, tails, skin (but no gills). Simmer, skimming, for 15 minutes. Strain through sieve and then through double thickness of wet cheesecloth.

Tomato pulp: Place tomatoes in boiling water for five seconds. Plunge immediately into cold water. Peel. Slice in half crosswise. With cut sides down, squeeze gently to remove seeds. Cut out cores. Dice flesh and drain 15-30 minutes in sieve.

Zest: This term refers to the minced peel of a citrus fruit. When preparing zest, peel the fruit thinly, avoiding the bitter white pith underneath.

ACKNOWLEDGEMENTS

The authors' heartfelt thanks to:

Alison Brown Cerier at Doubleday for her confidence and enthusiasm.

David Fuller at Evergreen Publishing for his patience and steadiness when lesser men would have trembled.

Ken Gouldthorpe and Knute Berger at Evergreen, whose support lay the foundation.

Judy Gouldthorpe, a copy editor and cook of surpassing knowledge and attention to detail.

Carrie Seglin and Elizabeth Watson for their photography and design skills so beautifully displayed herein.

Jayn Butt, Paul Irvin and Jacki Miles for their technical skills in the composition and layout of the text.

The friends and strangers who so willing shared their recipes and kitchen knowledge.

And, especially, to Juanita Walls, chief cook at The Wedge in Seattle, for her skilled assistance in testing recipes.

Photography & Art Credits

COVER
Carlan Tapp, food photographer
Charles Mauzy, scenic photographer
Phyllis Bogard, food stylist
Transparency: Duck Island Limited

STARTERS
Charles Krebs, 3
Jim Mears, 5
SOUPS
Charles Krebs, 17
Jim Mears, 19
SALADS
Gary Braasch, 29
Jim Mears, 31
PASTA
Charles Krebs, 41
Jim Mears, 43

SEAFOOD
Charles Krebs, 53
Jim Mears, 55
MEAT & POULTRY
Pat O'Hara, 73
Jim Mears, 75
SIDE DISHES
Gary Braasch, 91
Jim Mears, 93
DESSERTS
Charles Krebs, 103
Jim Mears, 105

Food Stylist: Phyllis Bogard
Prop Stylist: Deborah Currington
Calligraphy: Rosemary Woods
Illustrations: Jim Hays

TASTES *of the* PACIFIC NORTHWEST

WILLAPA BAY

Washington's Fertile Oyster Bed

A gull's screech rips the misty silence. Somewhere out there, at the mud flats' edge, rushing waters slow until they are still. Soon the estuary will draw back nourishment from the great Pacific.

Through the mist comes an odd sound. Slap, slap, slap. Then a human figure materializes, trudging this way. The shape becomes a boy. A boy wearing hip boots. Hip boots that meet with each stride. Slap, slap, slap. Behind him, more slaps. More boys wearing hip boots and slogging, single file, across mud the color of rich caramel.

The boys, six in number, as the mist grudgingly reveals, have come from harvesting oysters far out on the mud flats of Willapa Bay, in southwestern Washington. Tide turning, they have brought their orange baskets back to dry land, their labor over until the next tide change.

Smoking cigarettes, slurping coffee, they readily provide details: 38 cents a bushel when the picking is good. They dump their oysters in large tubs marked by buoys that are picked up by boat when the tide rises. It's hard work, but that's what they know, for they live on a slender spit called the Long Beach Peninsula that thrusts into the Pacific Ocean from the upper lip of the Columbia River's mouth, and the peninsula's business is mainly cranberries and oysters.

Willapa Bay is the last great estuary on the US West Coast that is still unpolluted. One hundred and ten acres

STARTERS

in area, half of which is exposed at low tide, the bay is one of the principal oyster-growing areas of the Pacific Northwest. Many such areas exist, from British Columbia south to the Oregon coast. Willapa Bay stands out, however, if only because of its history.

Once there were vast reefs of the native oyster, the tiny, delectable Olympia, here. When San Francisco was gripped by Gold Rush fever, oysters shipped there from Willapa Bay fetched a silver dollar apiece. A town named Oysterville sprang up on the peninsula almost overnight, and fabulous stories were told of its wealth.

Overharvesting, pests, freezing winters and–in other areas–pollution nearly killed off the native oyster early in this century all over the Pacific Northwest. Oysterville died as quickly as it had been born. The oyster industry survived only because of the importation of a large Japanese oyster, now called the Pacific.

Today, Pacifics dominate the region's oyster harvest. But Olympias are gradually making a comeback, and a Japanese oyster called the Kumamoto–smaller and sweeter than the Pacific–is becoming increasingly popular.

Willapa Bay never was forced completely out of the oyster business. While once it was concentrated on the peninsula side of the bay, though, now the mainland side is dominant. The northern half of the peninsula today draws visitors more than oystermen. Summer is the busiest season, but true romantics come in the winter, when Pacific storms kick up big winds and waves that pound at the ocean shore.

"We used to have a lot of oyster plants here," a peninsula native named Bud Goulter says. "Mom-and-pop plants, you know. Used to have 500 people in the Oyster Union. Now we don't have a union. Only about 100 people left in the business."

Some of those work in plants on a pier poking out over the bay at a place called Nahcotta, shucking, packing and smoking the oysters picked by the boys who slog over the mud flats. The shuckers work intently, and it's a long moment before one senses a visitor looking over her shoulder. She glances up from her work, a fat Pacific oyster glistening on the shell she has just opened. She holds up the shell for inspection. "Beautiful, huh?" she says.

"Are Willapa Bay oysters the best?" she's asked.

"Everybody has their favorite," she replies. "Around here, we like these. Willapa Bay oysters are known all over. That's good enough for me."

As succulent as their home along Washington's Willapa Bay is sublime (see overleaf), these Pacific oysters are perfectly complemented by a Seattle chef's award-winning sauces, one using soy sauce, sesame seeds and cilantro as a base, the other a simple blend of red wine vinegar, shallots and black pepper (recipe on page 8).

STARTERS

WALLA WALLA SWEET TART

This is one of the exceptions to the rule that Walla Walla Sweet onions from Washington should be served raw to show to best advantage. Their mild character comes through nicely in this preparation. Serve the tart as an appetizer or as part of a buffet.

> 6 medium Walla Walla Sweet onions,
>   quartered and sliced thinly
> ¼ cup butter
> 3 eggs, beaten lightly
> 1 cup crème fraîche (see Notes on
>   Ingredients, page xi)
> 1 tablespoon poppy seeds
>   Salt and pepper
> 2 tablespoons minced fresh dill
> ½ cup grated Gruyère cheese
>   9-inch tart shell, partly baked
> 1 tablespoon butter, cut in bits
> 2 tablespoons grated Parmesan

1. Sauté onions in butter over lowest heat until they are tender and golden brown, about 30 minutes. Cool.
2. Beat eggs with crème fraîche and poppy seeds. Salt and pepper to taste. Stir in dill. Stir in cooled onions and Gruyère.
3. Pour into tart shell. Sprinkle with Parmesan and dot with butter bits. Bake at 350°F for 40 minutes, or until knife inserted in center comes out clean and the tart is puffed and browned.

Serves 6-8

LAVOSH ROLLS WITH SMOKED TROUT PATÉ

Because of Idaho's pond-reared trout business, smoked trout is a familiar item in Pacific Northwest markets. Here it flavors rolls of the Armenian crackerbread called (among various spellings) lavosh. Sliced, these rolls make an excellent cold appetizer, buffet item or light lunch.

> 1 package large lavosh
> ½ pound smoked trout
> ⅓ cup butter, softened
> ½ pound cream cheese, at room
>   temperature
> 2 tablespoons minced scallion
> 2 tablespoons minced parsley
> 2 tablespoons minced fresh dill
> 1 tablespoon Dijon mustard
> 1 tablespoon lemon juice
>   Salt and pepper to taste
> 2 cucumbers, peeled and sliced paper
>   thin
> 4 small tomatoes, sliced paper thin

1. Submerge crackers in cold water for 10 seconds. Shake off excess water and place each one between sheets of oiled waxed paper. Stack damp lavosh sheets and place in bag for 2 hours to soften.
2. Cream trout, butter and cream cheese. Beat in all other ingredients except cucumbers and tomatoes.
3. To assemble, spread trout paté on crackers thickly, leaving 1-inch border along one edge. Arrange cucumber slices on paté close together without overlapping. Arrange tomato slices on cucumber without overlapping. Roll up cracker toward paté-free border. (Rolls should be compact but not so tight as to squeeze out filling.) Wrap in plastic wrap and refrigerate overnight.
4. Slice rolls diagonally 1½ inches thick, arrange on plates or platter and serve slightly chilled.

Makes 5 rolls

BAKED OYSTERS WITH GARLIC-PINE NUT BUTTER

No one has done more to draw attention to Pacific Northwest cooking than Jimella Lucas and Nanci Main. Their restaurant, The Ark, on Washington's Long Beach Peninsula, is a destination for visitors from across the country who appreciate fresh local ingredients and culinary creativity.

This simple appetizer features two of Lucas and Main's loves: oysters and garlic. If you have a shallow baking casserole large enough to hold the oysters, use it instead of a baking sheet and serve the oysters directly from the casserole.

    1½ cups butter, softened
    3 shallots, minced
    6 cloves garlic, minced
    ¾ cup pine nuts, toasted in a dry skillet
        and chopped
    ½ bunch parsley, chopped finely
    1 small bunch chives, chopped coarsely
        Juice of 1 lemon
    2 tablespoons brandy
        Pepper
    36 extra-small oysters on half shell
        Rock salt

1. Mix all ingredients except oysters and rock salt in blender or food processor until butter is smooth but still displays bits of dry ingredients. (Reserve 2 tablespoons pine nuts for garnish.)
2. Place oysters on bed of rock salt on baking sheet or in shallow baking casserole. Place dollop of butter mixture on each. Place in 375°F oven just until butter melts and oysters firm slightly. Garnish with reserved pine nuts and serve.

Serves 6

SALEH'S OYSTERS

Saleh Joudeh, owner-chef of Saleh al Lago in Seattle, like other immigrant cooks who come to the Pacific Northwest, was bowled over by the wonderful local ingredients. This is his homage to local oysters.

    16 fresh oysters
    1 tablespoon butter
    2 teaspoons flour
    ½ cup milk
        Pinch nutmeg
        Pinch cayenne pepper
        Salt
    2 tablespoons dry bread crumbs

1. Wash and shuck oysters, reserving bottom halves of shells and liquor from the shells. Place liquor in saucepan over low heat. Add oysters and cook 1-2 minutes, until they firm up slightly. Remove oysters with slotted spoon and reserve liquor.
2. Melt butter over medium-low heat in small saucepan. Add flour and cook, stirring, 1-2 minutes without browning. Slowly stir in milk and reserved oyster liquor. Stir in nutmeg, cayenne and salt (if desired). Remove from heat.
3. Dip oysters in sauce and spoon some sauce into reserved oyster shells. Place coated oysters in shells and sprinkle with bread crumbs. Arrange in shallow baking dish. Place under broiler as close as possible and broil 2 minutes.

Serves 4

**Oysters with
Two Sauces**

**Smoked
Salmon and
Marinated
Walla Walla
Sweets with
Sour Cream
Dressing**

OYSTERS WITH TWO SAUCES

Jacques Boiroux, chef at Seattle's Le Taste-vin restaurant, was one of the Young Toques who brought French cooking to Seattle during the World's Fair in 1962 and then stayed on to enrich the Pacific Northwest's culinary knowledge. Boiroux regularly wins contests with his seafood creations. These two dipping sauces for oysters, for example, garnered a blue ribbon in a state seafood festival.

Serve them with freshly shucked oysters on the half shell.

Sauce One

> $1/4$ cup light soy sauce
> 1 teaspoon sesame seeds, toasted in a
>   dry skillet
> 1 teaspoon minced cilantro
> 2 teaspoons rice vinegar
>   Few flakes red pepper

Combine ingredients and serve at room temperature.

Sauce Two

> $1/4$ cup red wine vinegar
> 2 teaspoons chopped shallots
> $1/2$ teaspoon freshly ground black pepper

Combine ingredients and serve at room temperature.

SMOKED SALMON AND MARINATED WALLA WALLA SWEETS WITH SOUR CREAM DRESSING

This attractive appetizer features two items for which the Pacific Northwest is renowned throughout the country: cold-smoked, or nova-style, salmon and the large sweet onions from Washington's Walla Walla Valley.

> 3 large Walla Walla Sweet onions, sliced
>   paper thin
> $1/2$ cup white wine vinegar
> $1/2$ cup water
> 2 tablespoons lemon juice
> $1/4$ cup sugar
> 1 tablespoon minced fresh dill
>   Salt and pepper
> 12 ounces smoked salmon, sliced thinly
>   Sour Cream Dressing (recipe
>   follows)
> 2 tablespoons capers, rinsed and
>   drained
>   Dill sprigs for garnish

1. Marinate onions in mixture of vinegar, water, lemon juice, sugar, dill and salt and pepper to taste for at least 3 hours.
2. Drain onions thoroughly. Mound them along one side of chilled serving plates. Arrange smoked salmon slices next to onions. Spoon Sour Cream Dressing over and garnish with capers and dill sprigs. Serve with pumpernickel bread.

Serves 6

Sour Cream Dressing

> 2 egg yolks
> 1 tablespoon cold water
> 1 cup vegetable oil
> 6 tablespoons white wine vinegar
> 2 cups sour cream
> 2 tablespoons lemon juice
>   Salt and white pepper
> 1 tablespoon minced fresh dill

Beat egg yolks with water in blender or food processor. With machine running, add half the oil in a thin, steady stream. Add vinegar and then the remaining oil. With machine still running, add sour cream, lemon juice and salt and pepper to taste. Stir in dill and chill.

Mussels and
Fennel in
Warm
Vinaigrette

Mussels with
Citrus-
Cilantro
Sauce

MUSSELS AND FENNEL IN WARM VINAIGRETTE

Pacific Northwest mussel fanciers frequently are caught in the vise of contradiction. On the one hand, locally cultivated mussels are world-class: plump, tender and mild-flavored. On the other hand, many fishmongers and restaurants here, suffering from ignorance and wildly inappropriate snobbery, don't offer local mussels. Instead, they proudly advertise "East Coast Mussels." The latter are wild, stronger flavored and, having been shipped a great distance, not as fresh as the local product.

Perhaps this odd situation arises from the fact that few Pacific Northwesterners ate mussels until fairly recently. Although wild mussels grow all around the region, they have found little favor among shellfish gatherers. Then in the mid-1970s, mussels began to be cultivated (grown suspended beneath rafts) in the waters of Penn Cove, off Whidbey Island in Washington's Puget Sound. Here are some of the world's finest mussel waters, drawing abundant nutrients from the Skagit River, which flows into the Sound nearby. Aficionados seek out Penn Cove mussels and are amply rewarded for their trouble. However, demand, much of it from outside the region, is beginning to outstrip supply as Penn Cove's fame spreads.

For now, there are enough mussels available to prepare this splendid appetizer, which requires lots of fresh bread to soak up the broth.

>   2 bulbs fennel, chopped coarsely
> 1/2 cup dry white wine
>   1 medium onion, halved lengthwise
>   and sliced thinly
>   1 sweet red pepper, sliced in 1/4-inch
>   strips
>   3 pounds mussels, bearded
>   Vinaigrette (recipe follows)

Simmer all ingredients except mussels for 2 minutes. Add mussels, cover pot and steam over high heat until mussels open, about 4-6 minutes. (Discard any that don't open.) Remove from heat. Pour liquid from pot through double layer of wet cheesecloth and reserve.

Cover pot to keep mussels warm while preparing vinaigrette.

Vinaigrette

>   3 tablespoons red wine vinegar
>   3 tablespoons lemon juice
>   2 cloves garlic, minced
> 1/2 cup olive oil
> 1/2 cup reserved liquid from steaming
>   mussels
> 1/2 cup chopped parsley
> 1/4 cup chopped cilantro
>   1 tablespoon capers, rinsed and drained
>   Salt and pepper

1. Mix vinegar, lemon juice and garlic. Whisk in olive oil. Whisk in warm mussel liquid. Stir in parsley, cilantro, capers and salt and pepper to taste.
2. Toss mussels and vegetables with vinaigrette and serve in warm bowls.

Serves 4-6

MUSSELS WITH CITRUS-CILANTRO SAUCE

Mussels make an excellent cold appetizer. These can also be presented as part of a buffet. The sauce combines the clean taste of cilantro, the sweet-acid flavor of citrus and the peppery zing of Tabasco.

>   2 egg yolks
>   2 tablespoons lemon juice
>   2 tablespoons orange juice
> 1/2 teaspoon salt
>   1 teaspoon Tabasco
> 1 1/2 cups olive oil
> 1/2 cup chopped fresh cilantro
>   2 dozen mussels, beards removed,
>   steamed open, removed from
>   shells and chilled

Mix egg yolks, citrus juices, salt and Tabasco in blender or food processor. With machine running, add oil in a thin, steady stream. Stir in cilantro. Chill several hours. Toss with mussels and serve.
Serves 4-6

CRAB-FILLED ARTICHOKE BOTTOMS WITH MORNAY SAUCE

Of the many Pacific Northwest culinary treasures, none is more precious than the Dungeness crab. Other regions might boast of their local crabs' virtues, but the Dungeness is the finest anywhere, with a full, deep flavor that needs no enhancing. Thus, you'll see no crab recipes in this book calling for loads of spices; those preparations are for thin-flavored crabs.

This dish, for instance, allows the crab flavor to come through the bland Mornay sauce. It's a classic appetizer, attractive and tasty, and fussy enough to demonstrate the effort that guests appreciate.

Artichoke Bottoms

6 *large artichokes*
2 *lemon wedges*
4 *cups water*
1/4 *cup lemon juice*
1 *teaspoon salt*
2 *tablespoons olive oil*

1. Snap off artichoke stems. Snap off tough outer leaves and cut off tender inner leaves. Trim remaining green parts with vegetable peeler. Rub exposed surfaces with lemon wedges to prevent discoloration.
2. Bring water, lemon juice, salt and olive oil to boil. Add artichokes and boil until tender, about 20 minutes. Remove artichokes and cool, reserving water. When cool enough to handle, remove chokes with spoon and return bottoms to cooking water to keep warm until ready to fill.

Crab Filling

1 *pound cooked Dungeness crabmeat*
1/4 *cup minced scallion*
1 *teaspoon minced fresh dill*
1 *tablespoon lemon juice*
Salt and pepper to taste

Mix all ingredients and set aside.

Mornay Sauce

1/4 *cup heavy cream*
1 *egg yolk*
1 1/2 *tablespoons butter*
1 1/2 *tablespoons flour*
1 1/2 *cups milk, scalded*
1/4 *cup grated Gruyère cheese*
1/4 *cup grated Parmesan*
Salt and white pepper
Pinch nutmeg

1. Beat cream and egg yolk until well combined.
2. Melt butter over medium-low heat in small saucepan. Stir in flour and cook 2 minutes, stirring constantly and taking care not to burn. Add milk and bring to gentle boil over medium-high heat while stirring. Lower heat and simmer 1 minute. Stir in Gruyère and half the Parmesan and cook, stirring, until cheeses melt. Salt and pepper to taste and add nutmeg. Remove from heat and beat in cream-egg mixture. Stir 1/4 cup sauce into crab mixture.

To assemble, line baking sheet with foil and butter it. Place warm artichoke bottoms on baking sheet and divide crab mixture among them. Spoon Mornay sauce over and sprinkle with remaining Parmesan. Broil 4 inches from heat for 4 minutes, until heated through and nicely browned.
Serves 6

WILD MUSHROOMS IN PHYLLO BASKETS

This first course is for those occasions when you want to put on a show in the dining room. The golden phyllo baskets filled with a savory melange of fresh and dried mushrooms and fresh herbs delight the eye and please the palate. Any fresh wild mushrooms will do, but a mixture of chanterelles and morels, when their seasons overlap, is especially good.

Phyllo Baskets

Frozen phyllo
Melted butter

1. Defrost phyllo by allowing to stand in refrigerator at least two days. Lay defrosted phyllo on waxed paper. Immediately cover with damp (not wet) towel and let stand 10 minutes to soften. Uncover phyllo, remove one sheet, lay on flat surface and cover again.
2. Brush both sides of phyllo sheet with melted butter. Cut into 6 equal pieces. Place buttered sheet into cup of muffin pan, allowing edges to spill over. Repeat with second sheet, turning 45 degrees and laying directly atop first. Continue making baskets until there are 12.
3. Bake at 350°F until lightly colored. Cool and remove from muffin pans.

2 ounces dried boletes (porcini in Italian markets)
2 cups hot water
2 shallots, minced
2 cloves garlic, minced
4 tablespoons butter
1 pound fresh wild mushrooms, sliced thinly
1/2 tablespoon minced fresh rosemary
1/2 tablespoon minced fresh thyme
1/2 cup port
1 tablespoon flour
3/4 cup heavy cream
Salt and pepper
2 tablespoons grated Parmesan
2 tablespoons butter, cut in bits

1. Soak dried boletes in hot water for 20 minutes. Drain (reserve strained liquid for flavoring soups or sauces), rinse, drain again, squeeze dry and chop coarsely.
2. Sauté shallots and garlic in butter over medium-low heat 2-3 minutes without browning. Add chopped dried boletes, fresh wild mushrooms, rosemary and thyme, raise heat to medium-high and cook until moisture has evaporated. Add port and cook, stirring, until it has evaporated. Sprinkle mushrooms with flour and stir until it has disappeared. Lower heat to medium, add cream and, stirring, boil until thick, 2-3 minutes. Salt and pepper to taste.
3. Spoon filling into baskets, sprinkle with Parmesan, dot with butter. Place baskets on baking sheet and bake at 400°F until filling is hot and bubbly, taking care not to over brown phyllo baskets. Serve immediately, two per person.

Serves 6

Herbed
Pancakes
with Wild
Mushroom
Butter

Brandied
Wild
Mushrooms
with Sour
Cream

HERBED PANCAKES WITH WILD MUSHROOM BUTTER

Pancakes as a first course? Why not? In France, they'd be called crêpes and be perfectly acceptable.

This is a lovely dish that should be followed by a light main course, perhaps a simple grilled or poached fish.

Pancakes

> 1 cup flour
> 1/4 cup minced onion
> 1 tablespoon minced parsley
> 1 tablespoon minced fresh herbs such
>   as basil, sage, thyme and
>   oregano
> 1/2 teaspoon salt
>   Pepper to taste
> 1 cup milk
> 2 eggs
> 1/2 cup soda water
>   Vegetable oil for frying

1. Mix flour, onion, parsley, herbs, salt and pepper in a large bowl. Make well in center.
2. Beat milk and eggs and pour into well in flour mixture. Blend with fork until smooth. Refrigerate batter for at least two hours.
3. Stir in soda water to thin batter (adding more, if necessary). Coat bottom of skillet with vegetable oil and preheat over medium-high heat. Ladle batter into skillet to form 3-inch pancakes. Cook until bottom is golden brown, flip and cook other side. Remove to plate in 200° F oven to keep warm.

Wild Mushroom Butter

> 2 cloves garlic, minced
> 3 tablespoons butter
> 1/2 pound wild mushrooms, cut in
>   1/4-inch-thick slices
>   Salt and pepper
> 4 ounces butter
> 1/4 cup minced parsley

1. Sauté garlic in the 3 tablespoons butter over medium-low heat 2 minutes, without browning. Add mushrooms, raise heat to medium and stir-fry 6-8 minutes, until they are tender. Salt and pepper to taste.
2. Melt the 4 ounces butter in small, heavy saucepan over medium-high heat and cook until browned but not burned.
3. To serve, divide pancakes among heated plates, spoon sautéed mushrooms on top, dribble browned butter over and sprinkle with parsley.

Serves 4-6

BRANDIED WILD MUSHROOMS WITH SOUR CREAM

Serve this cold appetizer before or with a meal of grilled meat, poultry or fish. Any wild mushroom, or combination of more than one, may be used.

> 1/4 cup minced onion
> 3 tablespoons olive oil
> 1 pound wild mushrooms, halved or
>   sliced if large
> 1/4 cup brandy
>   Salt and pepper
> 1 tablespoon lemon juice
> 1 cup sour cream
> 1 tablespoon minced parsley

1. Sauté onion in olive oil over medium-low heat until soft, about 2 minutes. Add mushrooms, raise heat to medium-high and sauté, stirring, until moisture has evaporated and mushrooms begin to brown.
2. Pour on brandy and, standing well away from pan, ignite and shake skillet until flames die. Remove from heat. Salt and pepper to taste.
3. Toss with lemon juice. Refrigerate at least 4 hours.
4. Mix with sour cream. Sprinkle with parsley and serve.

Serves 4

CHANTERELLE PUFFS WITH CRANBERRY KETCHUP

In the summer and autumn, when chanterelles are available, these make a splendid warm appetizer, with the tart-sweet ketchup serving as a foil to the earthiness of the mushrooms. When morels are available in the spring, they may be substituted for the chanterelles.

Cranberry Ketchup is an excellent condiment with turkey, smoked meats and even grilled salmon.

> 1 cup chicken stock (see Notes on
>   Ingredients, page xi)
> 1/2 pound chanterelles, chopped finely
> 4 tablespoons butter
> 1 teaspoon salt
> 1 cup flour
> 4 eggs
> 1/2 cup shredded smoked jack cheese
>   Cranberry Ketchup (recipe follows)

1. Bring chicken stock to boil. Lower heat to medium, add mushrooms, butter and salt. Whisk in flour and stir until dough becomes smooth and pulls away from sides of pan. Remove from heat. Beat in 1 egg at a time, making sure each is well incorporated before adding another. Beat in cheese.
2. Form puffs on oiled cookie sheet by dropping tablespoonfuls of dough 2 inches apart. Bake at 400°F for 10-12 minutes, until puffed and nicely browned. Serve warm with Cranberry Ketchup.

Serves 6-8

Cranberry Ketchup

> 1 cup coarsely chopped red onion
> 1 tablespoon orange zest
> 1/2 tablespoon lemon zest
> 2 tablespoons butter
> 1/2 cup raspberry vinegar
> 12 ounces cranberries
> 2 cups water
> 1 cup firmly packed dark brown sugar
> 1/2 teaspoon salt
> 1 teaspoon cinnamon
> 1/2 teaspoon allspice
> 2 teaspoons freshly grated ginger
>   Pinch ground cloves
> 1/4-1/2 teaspoon cayenne pepper according
>   to taste
> 1 1/2 tablespoons lemon juice

1. Sauté onion, orange zest and lemon zest in butter over medium-low heat until onion is quite soft, about 10 minutes. Add vinegar, cranberries and water. Raise heat to medium-high and bring to boil. Cook until cranberries pop.
2. Puree mixture in food mill or processor. Return puree to pot, stir in remaining ingredients except lemon juice and bring to boil. Turn heat to medium-low and simmer, stirring occasionally to prevent burning, for about 35 minutes, until the mixture is thick. Remove from heat, stir in lemon juice and chill before serving. (Will keep for a week tightly covered in refrigerator.)

Chanterelle
Tart

Fried
Cheddar with
Apple-Pear
Puree

CHANTERELLE TART

A wedge of this tart is a savory beginning to any meal. Or pair it with a green salad and serve for lunch or a light supper. Swiss cheese may be substituted for the smoked jack, but we like the slight smokiness with the earthy mushrooms. The tart's flavors emerge most fully when it is served warm, not hot.

>   2 shallots, minced
>   4 tablespoons butter
> $^1/_2$ pound chanterelles, cut in $^1/_4$-inch slices
>   Salt and pepper
>   2 tablespoons Madeira
>   3 egg yolks, lightly beaten
> 1 $^1/_4$ cups heavy cream
> $^1/_2$ cup shredded smoked jack cheese
> $^1/_4$ cup minced parsley
>   9-inch tart shell in pan with removable
>   bottom

1. Sauté shallots in butter over medium-low heat 2-3 minutes, until soft but not browned. Add mushrooms and salt and pepper to taste, raise heat to medium-high and cook until moisture has evaporated. Stir in Madeira and allow it to boil off. Set aside to cool slightly.
2. Beat egg yolks and cream. Stir in mushroom mixture, cheese and parsley. Pour into tart shell. Bake at 375° F for 25-30 minutes, until nicely browned.

Serves 6-8

FRIED CHEDDAR WITH APPLE-PEAR PUREE

This appetizer explores the affinity of fruit and cheese and presents a contrast between the warm cheese and chilled puree. The apples should be tart, perhaps Granny Smiths or Newtown Pippins (also called Newtons). Bartlett or Bosc pears will do equally well. The cheese slices shouldn't be thicker than $^3/_4$ inch to assure proper melting.

>   1 cup ground toasted hazelnuts (see
>   Notes on Ingredients, page xi)
> 1 $^1/_2$ cups dry bread crumbs
> 1 $^1/_2$ pounds extra-sharp cheddar, cut
>   in 6 pieces
>   1 cup flour
>   3 eggs, beaten
>   Vegetable oil for deep frying
>   Apple-Pear Puree (recipe follows)

1. Combine hazelnuts and bread crumbs. Dredge cheese pieces in flour, dip in beaten egg and roll in hazelnut-crumb mixture. Dip in egg again and roll again in nut-crumb mixture.
2. Deep-fry cheese in oil heated to 360° F, turning once, until just golden. Drain on paper towels, place on baking sheet and bake at 350° F for 4-5 minutes to insure even melting. Serve hot with Apple-Pear Puree.

Serves 6

Apple-Pear Puree

>   3 tart apples, peeled, cored and cut
>   into chunks
>   3 pears, peeled, cored and cut into
>   chunks
>   1 cup dry white wine
> $^1/_4$ cup Calvados or cognac
> $^1/_2$ cup packed light brown sugar
>   Pinch cinnamon
>   Pinch nutmeg
>   1 teaspoon dry mustard

Bring all ingredients to boil in a noncorrodible pot, turn heat to medium-low and simmer until fruit is very tender, 20-30 minutes. Cool slightly and puree in food mill or processor. Chill.

Asparagus-
Ham Paté
Wrapped in
Spinach

Asparagus
with Blue
Cheese Sauce

ASPARAGUS-HAM PATÉ WRAPPED IN SPINACH

Here's a colorful appetizer that makes a dramatic presentation when the Pacific Northwest's asparagus crop appears in the spring. Serve it with one of the region's dry white wines, such as Semillon Blanc.

The purpose of chilling certain ingredients and the blender or processor bowl is to create a light paté.

> 1-2 bunches spinach, stems removed
> 1 1/2 pounds asparagus
> 1/2 pound carrots, cut in 1/4-inch-thick sticks
> 1/2 pound ham, ground and chilled
> 1/4 pound chicken breast, ground and chilled
> 2 tablespoons lemon juice, chilled
> 3 egg whites, whipped lightly and chilled
> 1/2 cup olive oil, slightly chilled
> 1 teaspoon minced fresh tarragon
> Pinch nutmeg
> Salt and pepper

1. Blanch spinach in a few tablespoons of water brought to boil in a covered pot. Rinse in cold water, drain and pat dry in paper towels.
2. Snap woody ends off asparagus and peel stalks if tough. Blanch in boiling water for 2 minutes, rinse in cold water and drain.
3. Blanch carrots in boiling water for 40 seconds, rinse in cold water and drain.
4. Mix ground meats and lemon juice. In the chilled bowl of a blender or food processor, beat egg whites with meat mixture. With machine still running, add oil drop by drop. Mix in tarragon, nutmeg and salt and pepper to taste.
5. Butter a glass loaf dish. Line with spinach leaves. Spoon in one-quarter of the paté. Lay half the asparagus neatly on top. Top with one-quarter of the paté. Lay the carrots neatly on top. Top with one-quarter of the paté. Lay the remaining asparagus neatly on top. Top with remaining paté. (Lightly salt and pepper the vegetables as they are laid down.) Cover with spinach. Cover dish with buttered foil.
6. Place dish in a larger pan, then pour enough boiling water into pan to reach halfway up the sides of the dish. Bake at 325°F for 45 minutes. Remove dish from pan. Weight down paté with a flat surface that just fits inside dish, then place a heavy can or two on top of that. Refrigerate at least overnight.
7. To serve, remove foil, run a thin, sharp knife around the edges, taking care not to tear the spinach. Invert dish onto serving plate and paté should emerge. Slice and serve with Tomato Vinaigrette (recipe on page 48).

Serves 6

ASPARAGUS WITH BLUE CHEESE SAUCE

In season, it's hard to improve on a plate of asparagus as an appetizer. Some like their asparagus chilled. We favor room temperature so that the flavor comes through fully.

Many classic sauces serve asparagus well. This is one that features blue cheese, either an imported one such as Roquefort or a domestic such as the superb Oregon Blue (see page 24)

> 1 pound asparagus, woody ends snapped off, stalks peeled, steamed until tender and cooled

Blue Cheese Sauce

> 1 large clove garlic, peeled
> 1/2 teaspoon salt
> 1/2 teaspoon sugar
> 1/4 cup olive oil
> 2 tablespoons lemon juice
> 1 tablespoon minced onion
> 1/4 cup mashed blue cheese
> 1/2 cup sour cream

Sprinkle garlic with salt and sugar and mash with wooden spoon. Beat garlic into olive oil, lemon juice and onion. Stir in cheese and sour cream. Chill at least 1 hour before serving. Serve on room-temerature asparagus.

Serves 4-6

THE PALOUSE

Where No Furrow Runs Straight

The hills roll on and on. Treeless, their gentle contours seem sculpted, as if they were formed not by natural forces but by an unusually conscientious pastry chef. This is the Palouse, a region quite unlike any other, where the plow knows every acre but no furrow runs straight.

"Green lawn," as translated from the French, the Palouse comprises a 50-mile strip of eastern Washington and western Idaho, from the outskirts of Spokane to the Snake River Breaks. Once these hills produced little but wheat and other grains. Now those crops are widely rotated with dry peas and lentils, legumes that return to the soil the nitrogen that grains have drawn away. So congenial is the Palouse to dry peas and lentils, in fact, that virtually all of the nation's crop is harvested there.

Strange, even unearthly, to some, the Palouse exerts a powerful grip on those who farm it. John Carter, for instance, who jumps off a bulldozer he's using to clear drainage on one of his fields and climbs to the shoulder of Highway 95 just north of Tensed, Idaho.

"There are not many crop failures in the Palouse," Carter says with a smile, his lips shining neon-pink amid the dirt masking his face. Carter wipes his wire-rim glasses.

SOUPS

With them back in place and his thick strawberry-blond hair, Carter resembles John Denver. He's just as cheerful, too.

"I'm third generation on this land," he says. "I farm because I enjoy it so much. It's a love. My mother tells me she used to have to stop me from crawling after the tractors when they left for the fields."

Thirty-six years old, an agricultural economics graduate of the University of Idaho, Carter is the very model of a modern major farmer, discoursing easily about the chemical composition of his crops and the balance sheets he maintains in his farm-house office.

On his 1,100 acres, Carter raises all the Palouse's principal crops: wheat, barley, oats, dry peas, lentils and rapeseed. (Rapeseed produces oil, some industrial, some edible, depending on the variety of plant.) From early spring until winter snows blanket the Palouse, Carter watches the hills change from one color to the next. The greens of spring are interrupted in mid-May when the flowers of the towering rapeseed plants burst into brilliant yellow. Midsummer brings forth golden grains. In the fall, the greens return, as winter grain shoots emerge on the hillsides. "It is one of the prettiest places I've ever seen," Carter says, "and I've traveled a lot."

Unlike the semi arid regions of central Washington and Oregon, the Palouse is favored by a reliable rainfall, not sufficient to produce the fir and hemlock of the Pacific Northwest's coastal regions but ideal for certain grains and legumes. The prevailing weather comes from the southwest. But Palouse farmers are acquainted with all winds, including those that sweep down from the Arctic and drive the temperature to as low as minus 30° F. "There are times when I'm plowing," Carter says, "that I have to change directions three or four times in an hour because the wind shifts and I can't see where I'm going through the dust. You'll see half a dozen dust devils at a time dancing around these hills sometimes. Down in the South Palouse, the wind doesn't ever not blow."

Carter is one of the Palouse's leading advocates of the virtues of lentils. The homely lentil has been cultivated for 7,000 years and is esteemed in Europe, Asia and South America. In the US, however, lentils enjoy little popularity, in part because many cooks think they, like beans, require the troublesome step of soaking before cooking. They don't, however, just rinsing.

Out in the field, Carter doesn't even bother with that. "I like to eat them right out of the combine," he says. "Of course, they're a little hard on your teeth. They're tough little devils."

A truck rumbles past on the highway, the driver punching its horn. Carter waves. "A friend," he explains. "That's another thing about the Palouse. There are probably more hills than people, but the people who are here are the friendliest, most helpful anywhere. I can't think of another place I'd rather be."

The Pacific Northwest includes an astonishing variety of landscapes, from the Palouse region of eastern Washington and western Idaho (see overleaf) to the coastal valleys renowned for cheeses such as Oregon's Tillamook cheddar, here combined with broccoli to create a nourishing soup (recipe on page 23).

SOUPS

CIOPPINO ALLA NAPOLETANA

This seafood soup, disarmingly simple though it might appear, attracts an enthusiastic following at Carmine Smeraldo's restaurant, il Terrazzo Carmine, in Seattle. Prepared Naples-style, after Smeraldo's hometown, the soup is transformed into a sum greater than its parts. He serves it, in proper Italian style, as a first course. But many of his patrons make a meal of the soup by requesting repeated infusions of bread.

4 cloves garlic, chopped
1 cup olive oil
1 Dungeness crab, cut in 8 parts
8 large prawns in their shells
1 pound canned Italian tomatoes, chopped in their juice
1 cup dry white wine
1 tablespoon finely chopped parsley
2 large squid, cleaned and sliced in thin strips
1/2 pound halibut, cut in 2-inch chunks
1 pound mussels, beards removed
1 pound steamer clams
Salt and pepper

1. Sauté garlic in olive oil over medium heat for 30 seconds without browning. Add crab and prawns and sauté, stirring, for 1 minute. Add tomatoes and their juice, bring to boil, turn heat to medium-low, add wine and parsley and simmer 30 minutes.
2. Add squid and halibut and simmer 10 minutes more. Add mussels and clams, cover and steam until they open. (Discard those that don't open.) Salt and pepper to taste and serve.
Serves 6-8

OYSTER-SPINACH BISQUE

Chef Mark Finnigan of the Herald Street Caffe in Victoria, British Columbia, makes this popular soup by the gallon. He uses fresh local Pacific oysters and spoons a teaspoon of sherry into each bowl just before serving for taste and tantalizing aroma.

1 stalk celery, chopped finely
1 small onion, chopped finely
1 clove garlic, chopped finely
2 strips bacon, chopped finely
4 tablespoons butter
3 tablespoons flour
4 cups fish stock (see Notes on Ingredients, page xi)
10-12 medium freshly shucked oysters
1 tablespoon finely chopped fresh lemon thyme
1 bunch fresh spinach
1 teaspoon cayenne pepper
Salt and pepper
1 1/2 cups whipping cream
6 teaspoons dry sherry

1. Sauté celery, onion, garlic and bacon in butter over medium-low heat 8-10 minutes. Remove from heat and stir in flour to make roux.
2. Return to heat and add fish stock, oysters, lemon thyme, spinach, cayenne and salt and pepper to taste. Simmer until oysters firm up and are just cooked through. Puree in blender or food processor.
3. Return to heat, stir in cream and heat through. Serve immediately, adding a teaspoon of sherry to each bowl at the last moment.
Serves 8

SEAFOOD GAZPACHO

Most of the shrimp and scallops caught off the coast of the Pacific Northwest are taken by Oregon fishermen. When the shrimp are plentiful, the fishermen forsake scallops, which are more difficult to harvest. Nevertheless, this recipe assumes the availability of both. Serve it for lunch on a hot summer day or to begin an evening meal.

> 6 cups fish stock (see Notes on
>   Ingredients, page xi) or clam juice
> 1 cup dry white wine
> 1 onion, chopped coarsely
> ³/₄ pound uncooked shrimp, shelled
>   and deveined
> 1 pound sea scallops, halved
>   Salt and pepper
> 2 tablespoons lemon juice
> 3 tablespoons olive oil
> 6 large tomatoes, peeled and seeded
> 2 tablespoons olive oil
> ³/₄ pound cooked crabmeat
>   Vegetable Salsa (recipe follows)

1. Bring fish stock or clam juice, wine and onion to boil in a noncorrodible pan. Lower heat and simmer 15 minutes. Add shrimp and scallops and simmer 2 minutes, until scallops are opaque all the way through. Remove shrimp and scallops with slotted spoon, leaving onions in pan. Strain stock. Measure out 2 cups and boil to reduce by half. Chill in refrigerator. (Reserve leftover stock for another use.)
2. Mix salt and pepper to taste with lemon juice. Whisk in the 3 tablespoons olive oil. Toss mixture with the shrimp and scallops to coat. Refrigerate to chill, tossing periodically.
3. Puree tomatoes in blender, food mill or processor. Mix puree with the chilled fish stock, salt and pepper to taste and the 2 tablespoons olive oil. Mix with shrimp and scallops. Fold in crabmeat. Ladle into chilled soup plates and spoon on dollops of vegetable garnish.

Serves 6-8

Vegetable Salsa

> Salt and pepper
> 1 tablespoon lemon juice
> 2 tablespoons olive oil
> 1 green pepper, diced finely
> 1 red pepper, diced finely
> 1 cucumber, peeled, seeded and
>   diced finely
> 1 large red onion, diced finely
> 2 scallions, sliced thinly

Mix salt and pepper to taste with lemon juice. Whisk in olive oil. Toss with vegetables.

SALMON SOUP

When Scandinavian immigrants arrived in the Pacific Northwest, they found much that was familiar, including an abundance of salmon. Many of them almost certainly prepared some version of this soup, which is common in Scandinavia. It's hearty enough to serve as a main course.

> 4 cups fish stock (see Notes on
>   Ingredients, page xi)
> 5 boiling potatoes, peeled and diced
> 1 large onion, chopped coarsely
> 1 pound salmon, skin removed and
>   diced in ¹/₂-inch cubes
> 2 cups heavy cream
> 4 tablespoons butter, cut into bits
> ¹/₄ cup dry white wine
>   Salt and pepper
> ¹/₂ cup chopped fresh dill

Bring fish stock to boil with potatoes and onion. Lower heat and simmer, covered, about 20 minutes, until potatoes are tender. Add salmon and simmer 2 minutes. Add cream, butter, wine and salt and pepper to taste. Simmer until heated through. Add dill and serve.
Serves 4-6

Clam Broth
with Shrimp
Dumplings

Halibut
Bourride with
Aioli

CLAM BROTH WITH SHRIMP DUMPLINGS

The Pacific Northwest's melting pot contains many ethnic flavors. None is more pronounced, particularly in the region's western areas, than the Japanese. Here is a Japanese-style soup containing clams, wild mushrooms and shrimp, all local favorites. (The Dashi called for is a Japanese soup base, available in supermarkets and Asian food stores. Likewise the fish sauce.)

Broth

> 3 pounds clams
> 3 teaspoons Dashi, dissolved in
>   1 cup hot water
> 5 cups cold water
> 2 teaspoons Japanese fish sauce
> 2 tablespoons sake
> 2 teaspoons mild soy sauce

1. Place clams, Dashi and cold water in a covered soup pot and bring to boil. As soon as clams open, remove with a slotted spoon. (Discard clams that don't open.) Remove clams from shells, saving 12 in shells for garnish, and reserve.
2. Strain broth through sieve lined with wet cheesecloth, leaving sand in bottom of pot. Rinse cheesecloth and replace in sieve for later use. Rinse pot. Return broth to pot. Season with fish sauce, sake and soy sauce. Salt broth if necessary.

Dumplings

> 1/2 pound uncooked shrimp, shelled and
>   deveined
> 1 teaspoon sake
>   Pinch salt
> 1/2 teaspoon grated fresh ginger
> 1 egg white

1. Puree shrimp in a food processor or mince to a paste. If using processor, include sake and salt. If mincing with a knife, beat in sake and salt after shrimp paste has been placed in a bowl.

2. Stir in ginger. Beat egg white until just foamy. Fold into shrimp mixture.
3. Moisten hands with cold water and shape shrimp mixture into 12 balls between palms of hands.
4. Bring clam broth to strong simmer. Poach dumplings 4 at a time in broth. They are done when they rise to the top. Remove with slotted spoon and reserve in warm bowl.
5. Strain broth again through sieve lined with wet cheesecloth. Return broth to simmer.

Garnish

> 2 matsutake mushroom caps, sliced 1/4
>   inch thick
>   Green ends of 2 scallions, thinly
>   sliced on the diagonal

To serve, divide clams, clams in shells and dumplings among 6 soup bowls. Divide mushroom and scallion slices also. Pour on hot broth and serve.
Serves 6

HALIBUT BOURRIDE WITH AIOLI

A cousin to bouillabaisse, bourride is distinguished from that more celebrated Mediterranean soup by the inclusion of the garlic mayonnaise the French call aioli. Many types of fish may be included in bourride, but what could be finer than snowy-white halibut from the cold Pacific?

> 4 Russet potatoes, peeled and sliced 1/4
>   inch thick
> 4 large tomatoes, peeled, seeded and
>   chopped coarsely
> 3 onions, peeled and sliced 1/3 inch thick
> 1 1/2 cups clam juice
> 1/3 cup olive oil, extra-virgin if possible
> 1 tablespoon fennel seeds
> 1 teaspoon stem saffron
>   Salt and pepper
> 4 pounds halibut, in 2-inch cubes
> 6-8 large croutons (see note)
>   Aioli (recipe follows)

1. Place potato slices in large enameled pot, top with chopped tomato and then onion slices. Add clam juice and

enough cold water to cover by 3 inches.
Dribble in olive oil, add fennel seeds
and saffron. Let stand 2 hours at room
temperature.

2. Bring soup to boil, lower heat and simmer about 8 minutes, until potatoes are
almost tender. Salt and pepper to taste.
Add halibut pieces, bring to boil again,
lower heat and simmer about 5 minutes.
Do not overcook. Halibut is cooked
when it's opaque all the way through.
Remove from heat, cover and allow to
rest 10 minutes.

3. To serve, place crouton on bottom of
soup plate, spoon a generous dollop of
aioli on crouton, ladle in a portion of
fish, vegetables and broth.

Serves 8-10

Aioli

> ¹/₂ cup stale French bread crumbs
> 3 tablespoons white wine vinegar
> 8 cloves garlic, chopped coarsely
> 1 egg yolk
> ¹/₂ teaspoon salt
> 1 - 1 ¹/₂ cups olive oil, extra-virgin if possible
> 3 tablespoons hot broth from the bourride
> 3 tablespoons lemon juice

1. Soak bread crumbs in wine vinegar 10
minutes. Squeeze out liquid.

2. Puree bread crumbs and garlic in a
mortar with a pestle until smooth. Add
egg yolk and salt and work them into
puree. Transfer mixture to a small bowl.

3. Blend in olive oil with a wooden spoon
drop by drop until mixture is more
pliable. Switch to whisk and, whisking
constantly, add olive oil in a thin,
steady stream.

4. Thin mixture with hot broth and lemon
juice. (Aioli should be quite thick,
thicker than, for instance, mayonnaise.
It can be prepared in a blender or food
processor, but it would not have the
same texture and gloss as with the
above, original method.)

Note: *To make croutons, slice French or
Italian bread, butter slices (or brush both sides
with olive oil) and toast in a 325° F oven until
lightly browned.*

BROCCOLI-TILLAMOOK CHEDDAR SOUP

No Pacific Northwest cheese has a more
familiar name than Tillamook cheddar
from Tillamook County, Oregon. The dairy
farmers' co-op there has been producing
cheese for nearly a century. Tillamook
cheddar, which ages smooth and soft as op-
posed to the English-style dry and crumbly
cheddars of Vermont and New York, is in
such demand on the West Coast that little
of it ages to the ideal state. An aged Tillamook wouldn't show to best advantage in
this soup, though it would lend it distinction. Best, perhaps, to save a rare aged Tillamook to close the meal this soup opens.

> 1-2 heads broccoli
> 1 bunch watercress, stems removed
> 5 cups chicken stock (see Notes on
> Ingredients, page xi)
> 5 tablespoons butter
> 4 tablespoons flour
> 1 cup milk
> 2 cups heavy cream
> 1 pound sharp Tillamook cheddar,
> grated
> Salt and pepper
> 2 tablespoons Worcestershire sauce
> ¹/₄ cup sherry

1. Peel the stems of the broccoli and chop
coarsely. Break tops into 1-inch-long
flowerets. Place broccoli and watercress
in soup pot with 3 cups of the chicken
stock. Bring to boil, lower heat and
simmer 5 minutes.

2. Melt butter over medium-low heat in
small, heavy saucepan. Stir in flour and
cook 2 minutes, stirring constantly and
taking care not to brown. Gradually add
milk and cream and bring to gentle boil
while stirring. Lower heat and simmer
5 minutes.

3. Add cream sauce to broccoli. Add
remaining 2 cups chicken stock and
bring to boil. Lower heat, add cheddar
and stir occasionally as cheese melts.
Salt and pepper to taste. Stir in Worcestershire sauce and sherry. Serve hot.

Serves 6-8

Broiled
Tomato Soup
with Oregon
Blue Cheese

Essence of
Wild
Mushroom
Soup with
Pistou

BROILED TOMATO SOUP WITH OREGON BLUE CHEESE

One of the Pacific Northwest's most renowned cheeses is a blue produced by the Rogue River Valley Creamery in Central Point, Oregon, near Medford. Oregon Blue is such a distinctive cheese–cream-colored, with a dark blue mold–that we have included it in several recipes. Its presence here elevates an excellent tomato soup onto a higher plane.

>3 pounds tomatoes, peeled, halved
>   horizontally and seeded
>1 tablespoon sugar
>1 onion, chopped coarsely
>2 garlic cloves, minced
>1 tablespoon butter
>1 tablespoon flour
>4 cups chicken stock (see Notes on
>   Ingredients, page xi)
>1/3 pound Oregon Blue cheese
>8 ounces cream cheese
>2 tablespoons tomato puree
>1 cup loosely packed basil leaves, cut
>   in thin strips
>   Salt and pepper
>1/4 cup grated Parmesan cheese

1. Place tomato halves, cut side up, on baking sheet. Sprinkle with sugar. Place 5 inches below broiler and broil until sugar begins to brown. Take care not to burn. Cut out tomatoes' cores.
2. Sauté onion and garlic in butter over medium-low heat until soft, about 10 minutes. Stir in flour until no trace remains. Add tomatoes, chicken stock, blue cheese, cream cheese, tomato puree, basil and salt and pepper to taste. Bring to boil, lower heat and simmer until slightly thickened, about 1 hour. Strain. Rewarm. Ladle into soup plates, sprinkle with grated Parmesan and serve.

Serves 4-6

ESSENCE OF WILD MUSHROOM SOUP WITH PISTOU

Although this soup can be prepared with many kinds of wild mushrooms, or even cultivated button mushrooms, the choice here are boletes, or *Boletus edulis*. Boletes, called *porcini* in Italy and *cepes* in France, enjoy an exalted status in cooking. Firm and meaty, boletes can be treated like steak: sliced thickly, brushed with olive oil and grilled on the backyard barbecue. In this case, they contribute their distinctive wild flavor to a meat broth for a first-course soup. The best place to find boletes is in their natural habitat, the forest. But some markets in the Pacific Northwest now carry them fresh, at prices appropriate to their culinary station.

This soup profits greatly from the best possible ingredients. Use a good-quality tomato paste, a fruity extra-virgin olive oil and imported Parmigiano Reggiano (the original and still finest Parmesan), and the rewards will be worth the price.

>1 onion, sliced thinly
>2 tablespoons butter
>2 tablespoons olive oil
>1 pound boletes, chopped coarsely
>   (reserve 12 thin slices for
>   garnish)
>1 1/2 quarts strong meat stock (see Notes on
>   Ingredients, page xi)
>   Salt and pepper
>6 croutons (see note)
>   Pistou (recipe follows)
>   Parmesan cheese

1. Sauté onion in butter and olive oil over very low heat until caramel-brown, about 30 minutes. (Take care not to burn.)
2. Add mushrooms, including garnish slices, raise heat to medium-low and sauté, stirring, for 5 minutes. Remove garnish slices and reserve.
3. Place mushrooms and meat stock in soup pot. Bring to boil, lower heat and simmer 30 minutes. Strain through cheesecloth-lined sieve, return to pot and bring to simmer until ready to serve. Salt and pepper to taste.

**Chilled Fresh
Pea Soup
with
Cucumber-
Mint
Chutney**

4. To serve, ladle soup into bowls, spoon a dollop of pistou on each crouton, float croutons on soup and garnish with reserved mushroom slices. Pass extra pistou and Parmesan at the table.

Serves 6

Pistou

> 6 cloves garlic, minced
> 1/4 cup tomato paste
> 1/2 cup finely chopped fresh basil
> 1 cup grated Parmesan cheese
> 1/2 cup olive oil

Combine garlic, tomato paste, basil and Parmesan and whisk in olive oil. Cover and let stand at room temperature for 2 hours, or longer if refrigerated. Bring to room temperature before serving.

Note: *To make croutons, slice French or Italian bread, butter slices (or brush both sides with olive oil) and toast in a 325° F oven until lightly browned.*

CHILLED FRESH PEA SOUP WITH CUCUMBER-MINT CHUTNEY

Washington's Yakima River Valley is the premier mint-growing region in the country. That crop is sold commercially. As any Pacific Northwest homeowner knows, however, fresh mint is readily available in the backyard, even if it isn't cultivated.

The fresher the peas, the better is this soup. Try it for a light lunch on a hot summer day. Or serve it as a first course for dinner.

> 1 small onion, chopped finely
> 2 tablespoons unsalted butter
> 8 sprigs watercress, stems removed
> 1 large cucumber, peeled, seeded and chopped
> 3 cups fresh peas
> 3 cups chicken stock (see Notes on Ingredients, page xi)
> Salt and white pepper
> 1 1/2 cups heavy cream
> 1 tablespoon finely chopped fresh mint Cucumber-Mint Chutney (recipe follows)

1. In large, heavy saucepan or soup pot, sauté onion in butter over medium-low heat until soft but not brown, about 10 minutes. Add watercress and cucumber and cook about 2 minutes, until watercress wilts.
2. Add peas, chicken stock and salt and white pepper to taste. Bring to boil, turn heat to low and simmer, partly covered, until peas are tender, about 10 minutes.
3. Strain soup, reserving liquid. Puree solids, with a little liquid, in food mill. Combine puree with reserved liquid.
4. Stir in cream and mint. Chill, covered, thoroughly. Serve chilled with a dollop of Cucumber-Mint Chutney.

Serves 6-8

Cucumber-Mint Chutney

> 1 large cucumber, peeled, seeded and chopped finely
> 1 cup loosely packed fresh mint leaves, chopped finely
> 1 teaspoon cumin
> 1/2 cup unflavored yogurt
> 1/2 cup sour cream
> Lemon juice

Combine ingredients and chill thoroughly. Bring to room temperature before serving.

POTATO, PEAR AND CELERY SOUP

Austrian-born Peter Schott, owner-chef of the restaurant bearing his name in the Idanha Hotel in Boise, Idaho, says "there is no finer potato anywhere" than Pacific Northwest Russets. He's devised many soups exploiting the potato, including this unusual combination. Don't hesitate to try it. The classically trained Schott enjoys an excellent reputation because he knows how to blend flavors and make use of local ingredients. Any variety of pear will do.

> 3 tablespoons finely diced shallots
> 3 tablespoons finely diced onion
> 5 tablespoons unsalted butter
> 2 medium Russet potatoes, peeled and cut in $^1/_2$-inch cubes
> 2 medium pears, peeled, cored and cut in $^1/_2$-inch cubes
> 3 stalks celery, cut in $^1/_2$-inch cubes
> 5 cups chicken stock (see Notes on Ingredients, page xi)
> 1 cup heavy cream
> Salt to taste
> $^1/_8$ teaspoon white pepper
> $^1/_8$ teaspoon nutmeg

Garnish

> 1 medium Russet potato, peeled and cut in $^1/_2$-inch cubes
> 2 stalks celery, cut in $^1/_2$-inch cubes
> 2 cups chicken stock
> 1 medium pear, peeled, cored and cut in $^1/_2$-inch cubes

1. Sauté shallots and onion in butter over medium heat in heavy-bottomed saucepan until translucent, about 5 minutes. Add potatoes, pears and celery and sauté 5 minutes. Add chicken stock and simmer 20 minutes.
2. Puree soup in blender or food processor. Return to saucepan and reheat. Add cream. Add salt, white pepper and nutmeg.
3. Meanwhile, prepare garnish by simmering potato and celery in chicken stock until tender, 10-15 minutes. Add pear and simmer 1-2 minutes to heat through. Stir garnish into soup just before serving.

LENTIL SOUP

This soup seems to taste better if it's made a day ahead and allowed to sit in the refrigerator overnight. In that case, don't add the cream until it's been reheated and ready to serve. (The 5-Star Spice can be found in Asian food stores.)

> $^1/_4$ pound pancetta or unsliced bacon, sliced in $^1/_4$-inch batons
> 1 onion, sliced thinly
> 2 medium carrots, cut in $^1/_4$-inch cubes
> 2 cloves garlic, minced
> 2 tablespoons chopped fresh herbs, such as thyme, oregano, sage and parsley
> 1 cup lentils, rinsed and drained
> 6 cups chicken stock (see Notes on Ingredients, page xi)
> Pinch cardamom
> $^1/_4$ teaspoon 5-Star Spice
> $^1/_2$ cup heavy cream

1. Sauté pancetta or bacon in heavy saucepan or soup pot over medium-low heat until it renders its fat and begins to brown a bit. Add onion, carrots, garlic and fresh herbs. Sauté, stirring, until onion is limp, about 10 minutes.
2. Add lentils and chicken stock. Bring to boil, lower heat, add spices and simmer until lentils are tender but not falling apart, about 30 minutes. (Add more stock if needed.)
3. Ladle about one-third of the soup–more lentils than liquid–into blender or food processor and puree. Return to soup. Add cream, reheat gently and salt and pepper, if necessary.

Serves 4-6

Roasted
Garlic and
Potato Soup

Chilled
Asparagus
Soup with
Fresh Dill

ROASTED GARLIC AND POTATO SOUP

A fierce argument periodically erupts between Idaho and Washington as to which state produces the finer potatoes. The subjective issue will never be resolved. Objectively, Idaho produces more, Washington produces more per acre. As far as the rest of the country is concerned, however, the interstate rivalry is immaterial. All that matters is that Pacific Northwest baking-type potatoes are unequaled anywhere. Big, solid Pacific Northwest Russets are high in nutrition, low in price and versatile in the kitchen.

Don't be dismayed by the amount of garlic called for in this soup. Roasting mellows garlic. The result is a rich, nutty flavor without harshness.

> Cloves of 3 heads garlic, peeled
> 1 cup olive oil
> 3 sprigs fresh thyme
> 6 leaves fresh sage
> 1 1/2 quarts chicken stock (see Notes on Ingredients, page xi)
> 1 pound Russet potatoes, peeled and cut in 1/2-inch cubes
> 1 cup milk
> 1 cup heavy cream
> Cayenne pepper
> Salt and pepper

1. Toss garlic with olive oil to coat well. Toss with thyme and sage and place in heavy baking pan. Cover pan with foil and bake at 275°F for 20 minutes. Remove foil and continue baking until garlic is quite soft. Do not allow garlic to brown very much. Remove herbs and all except 2 tablespoons of oil. (Reserve oil for another use: coating croutons, for instance.)
2. Bring chicken stock to boil. Add potatoes, lower heat and simmer strongly until tender. Add garlic and oil and simmer 10 minutes.
3. Puree soup in blender or food processor. Return to soup pot, bring to boil, add milk and cream, and cayenne pepper, salt and pepper to taste.

Serves 6-8

CHILLED ASPARAGUS SOUP WITH FRESH DILL

As in physics, simplicity in cooking often equals elegance. That's the virtue of this soup, which features the straightforward flavor of fresh asparagus enhanced by fresh herbs. It can be served hot as well as cold, which makes it ideal for spring in the Pacific Northwest, when the weather is unpredictable. Ever optimistic, we offer it here in the chilled version.

> 2 pounds asparagus
> 2 cups chopped onion
> 6 tablespoons butter
> 6 cups chicken stock (see Notes on Ingredients, page xi)
> 1/4 cup chopped parsley
> 1 tablespoon minced fresh dill
> 2/3 cup heavy cream
> Salt and white pepper

1. Cut tips from asparagus and reserve. Snap off woody ends of stalks and discard. Peel stalks if tough and cut into 1-inch pieces.
2. Sauté onion in butter over low heat for 15 minutes, until very soft. Combine with chicken stock in heavy pot and bring to boil. Add asparagus stalks, cover, lower heat and simmer 45 minutes.
3. In blender or food processor, puree asparagus in stock along with parsley and dill. Press through sieve to remove any fibers.
4. Return soup to pot, add asparagus tips and simmer until tips are tender, about 6 minutes.
5. Stir in cream and salt and white pepper to taste. Remove from heat and chill before serving.

Serves 4-6

HOOD RIVER VALLEY

Pear Capital of the World

The locals snickered when Hans Lage bought himself a piece of the Hood River Valley for $300 and a shotgun. There weren't many locals in 1876, when Lage arrived at the end of the Oregon Trail, but the few there were reckoned that the German immigrant was plumb crazy to pay such a steep price. Well, Lage had the last laugh, all right, one that still echoes in the valley today, more than a century later.

The Lages, you see, are still there, working the land Hans purchased. Of course, the family plot has grown some. Now the Lages have 300 acres of the prettiest orchards you can imagine. They grow Red Delicious and Newtown Pippin apples and Bartlett, Anjou, Bosc and Comice pears. They pack and store their fruit in huge windowless buildings. And they plant trees that will still be bearing fruit 40 or 50 years from now, when future generations of Lages take pleasure and prosperity from the valley Hans discovered at the end of his rainbow.

The Hood River Valley isn't large–a scant 17 miles long by eight miles wide–but it is one of the great tree-fruit centers of North America. Beautiful, too. Falling down from the slopes of Mount Hood, it twists and turns until it intersects the grand Columbia River Gorge, always providing a view of the snowy pinnacle at its head.

SALADS

Mount Hood remains steadfast, unchanging, but the valley has seen many changes. Farmers and orchardists were in the minority among the early settlers. Lumber and dairy businesses formed the economic base at first, but the valley was ideal for growing tree fruits, and the orchards gradually took over. Today, they swoop down from the valley's steep sides right up to, and even around, the orchardists' houses. Most Pacific Northwest fruit-growing valleys tend to shelter other crops, too, but the Hood River Valley is pure tree fruit.

Apples used to be paramount. The demand for pears has increased in America, however, and no place grows better pears than the Hood River Valley. Today, two-thirds of the orchards produce pears. Foremost among them is the Anjou, a thin-skinned, spicy variety that doesn't cook well but is superb for eating fresh out of hand and slicing into salads. Anjou is a winter pear, meaning it withstands cold storage after autumn picking and therefore can be released for sale right through the winter. (Bartletts store poorly and usually are gone from the market by early December. All commercially significant pears other than Bartletts are called winter pears.) Second to Anjou among the valley's winter pears is the Bosc, a russeted pear with a long, graceful neck and curved stem. Boscs cook beautifully, and their elegance makes them ideal for poaching and serving whole. Trailing these two by a fair distance is the wondrous Comice. The last, however, shall be first.

"They're the Cadillac of pears," Eddie Lage, great-grandson of Hans, says. "My dad loved Comice. He used to keep a bucket of them in the engine room to ripen. Every morning he'd have two for breakfast."

County agent Dave Burkhardt agrees with Lage's opinion of Comice. "But," he goes on, "they're so hard to get to market in prime shape. They're susceptible to limb-rub (bruises from growing against limbs) and punctures when they're picked. They require careful handling, so a lot of people stay away from them."

Properly ripened, a Comice is fragrant, overflowing with sweet juice and buttery in texture. The way to eat a Comice, as Eddie Lage's father knew, is to slice it horizontally and scoop out the creamy flesh with a spoon.

Because they're tricky to grow and harvest, few orchardists bother with them. Nearly all of North America's Comice production, in fact, is in the Pacific Northwest, primarily in southern Oregon's Rogue River Valley. Eddie Lage readily acknowledges the rival valley's dominance when it comes to Comice. "It's a little warmer down there," he says. "But we can grow them here, too. When it comes to pears, this valley is the best in the world."

Creating harmony out of contrasting elements— such as in this unusual salad of pears, lettuce, arugula, red onions and prosciutto (recipe on page 32)—is a specialty of Pacific Northwest chefs, who seem to take their lead from an environment in which Oregon's snow-capped Mt. Hood towers above the fecund Hood River Valley (see overleaf).

SALADS

Poached Pear
Salad with
Raspberry
Vinaigrette

Pear, Snow
Pea and
Warm Goat
Cheese Salad
with Lime-
Mint
Dressing

POACHED PEAR SALAD WITH RASPBERRY VINAIGRETTE

Pears poached in red wine make an excellent dessert. To ensure that they cook evenly, choose pears of equal ripeness. They shouldn't be too soft, but they must be ripe to develop full flavor and proper texture. Oddly, pears don't mature properly if allowed to ripen on the branch; a tree-ripened pear usually is gritty. Picked green, stored cold for a month or more and ripened in the kitchen, they become buttery and juicy. Ripen them at room temperature. Placing pears in a paper bag, which concentrates the ripening agent, speeds the process. For poaching, Bartletts and Boscs are best.

The arugula called for is an Italian green with a peppery, bitter flavor. It's being cultivated now in this country and often can be found in supermarkets during the summer and autumn. Arugula and black pepper combine for a perfect counterpoint to the wine-poached pears. Freshly crushed pepper, always advisable, seems essential here.

> ½ head green leaf lettuce
> 1 bunch arugula
> 2 bulbs Belgian endive
> ½ small red onion, sliced thinly
>   Raspberry Vinaigrette (recipe follows)
> 18 thin slices prosciutto
>   Poached pears, sliced in eighths
>   (recipe follows)
> ¾ cup crème fraîche (see Notes on
>   Ingredients, page xi)
>   Freshly crushed black pepper

1. Tear lettuce and arugula. Trim core from endive and separate leaves. Toss with onion and vinaigrette.
2. On each chilled plate, lay out 3 slices prosciutto in spoke-wheel fashion. Divide greens among plates and mound. Arrange 4 pear slices around base of each mound of greens and 4 slices atop each mound. Place dollop of crème fraîche on pears. Crush generous amount of black pepper over all and serve.

Serves 6

Raspberry Vinaigrette

> ¼ cup raspberry vinegar
> 2 tablespoons balsamic vinegar
> 1 tablespoon lemon juice
>   Salt and pepper
> 1 cup olive oil
> ¼ cup pureed raspberries

Mix vinegars, lemon juice and salt and pepper to taste. Whisk in olive oil. Stir in raspberry puree.

Poached Pears

> 6 pears, peeled, cored and quartered
> 2 cups red wine
>   Peel of 1 lemon

Place pears, wine and lemon peel in saucepan and bring to boil. Lower heat, cover and simmer 10-30 minutes (depending on pears' ripeness), until pears are pierced easily with a knife. Remove with slotted spoon, drain and chill.

PEAR, SNOW PEA AND WARM GOAT CHEESE SALAD WITH LIME-MINT DRESSING

When inventive American chefs made cooking fun, even playful, one of the joys they discovered was re-creating the idea of the salad. Once served primarily as an accompaniment to a meat-and-potatoes meal, the salad has become a meal unto itself. The fun is in devising combinations that please the palate and the eye.

Here, Pacific Northwest pears are joined by snow peas of Asian origin and the red-cabbage-like radicchio prized by Northern Italians. Green, egg-shaped Anjou pears, mild and slightly spicy, are excellent for salads that call for uncooked pears.

Smoked
Chicken and
Wild Green
Salad with
Pear
Vinaigrette

¹/₂-pound head radicchio
1 bunch watercress, stems removed
   Heart of 1 medium head curly endive
1 head butter lettuce
2 pears, peeled, cored and sliced thinly
30 snow peas, trimmed, blanched and
   sliced in half diagonally
   Lime-Mint Dressing (recipe follows)
6 rounds goat cheese, marinated in
   olive oil several hours
1 cup fine, dry bread crumbs
¹/₂ cup pine nuts, toasted lightly in
   dry skillet

1. Tear greens and toss with pears, snow peas and dressing.
2. Roll marinated goat cheese rounds in bread crumbs, place on oiled baking sheet and bake at 400°F for 5 minutes.
3. Arrange greens on serving plates, place warm cheese rounds on top, sprinkle with pine nuts, drizzle with additional dressing and serve immediately.

Serves 6

Lime-Mint Dressing

¹/₂ cup lime juice
¹/₂ cup honey
   Salt and pepper
¹/₂ cup walnut oil
1 cup vegetable oil
1¹/₂ cups mint leaves, chopped finely

Mix lime juice, honey and salt and pepper to taste. Whisk in oils and mint.

SMOKED CHICKEN AND WILD GREEN SALAD WITH PEAR VINAIGRETTE

Wild greens thrive in cool, moist parts of the Pacific Northwest. Gathering them takes time and expertise. But they have become so popular in restaurants and home kitchens that many specialty markets now carry them mixed in bags. On menus and in markets, these mixtures often appear as "seasonal greens." Given such demand, the greens no longer are truly wild but are cultivated by small farmers.

Many types of greens will suit this salad, among them the peppery arugula; celery-flavored lovage; aptly named lemon balm; apple mint; mâche, also called corn salad; tart purslane. Add fresh herbs such as basil and dill to the salad and fill it out, if desired, with common greens such as green leaf and romaine lettuce.

Perhaps because of its long association with smoked salmon, which originated with the coastal Indians, the Pacific Northwest has many small producers of smoked meats and poultry. We like smoked chicken with these greens. The Pear Vinaigrette gives the right touch of sweet-sourness to the salad.

   Selection of wild greens
   Pear Vinaigrette (recipe follows)
¹/₂ pound smoked chicken, shredded

Toss greens with Pear Vinaigrette. Divide on serving plates and scatter with smoked chicken.
Serves 4

Pear Vinaigrette

1¹/₂ pears, peeled, cored and quartered
2 cups water
2 teaspoons sugar
2 tablespoons honey
¹/₂ cup raspberry vinegar
2 tablespoons Dijon mustard
2 tablespoons lemon juice
1 tablespoon minced fresh marjoram
1 cup vegetable oil
   Salt and white pepper

1. Simmer pears in water and sugar until tender, about 7 minutes. Cool in syrup. Remove pears and reserve syrup.
2. Puree pears in food mill or processor. Blend in honey, vinegar, mustard, lemon juice, marjoram and 4 tablespoons of the poaching liquid. Place in blender or food processor and, with machine running, mix in vegetable oil. Salt and pepper to taste.

APPLE, CELERY AND SMOKED JACK SALAD WITH POPPY SEED DRESSING

Golden Delicious apples are ideal for this salad, which constitutes a lunch by itself. Serve it, as suggested, on curly endive or any other green.

> 3 apples, peeled and cored
> Celery
> Smoked jack cheese
> Poppy Seed Dressing (recipe follows)
> Curly endive
> 1/4 cup toasted walnuts, chopped
>   coarsely

Cut equal amounts of apple, celery and smoked jack in 1/4-inch-thick sticks. Toss with dressing, serve on torn curly endive, with walnuts sprinkled on top.
Serves 4-6

Poppy Seed Dressing

> 2 eggs
> 2 tablespoons sugar
> 1/2 cup hot-sweet mustard
> 1/4 cup berry vinegar
> 1/4 cup red wine vinegar
> 2 cups vegetable oil
> 1 tablespoon poppy seeds
> Salt
> Coarsely ground black pepper

Beat eggs, sugar, mustard and vinegars in blender or food processor until well blended. With machine running, add oil in thin, steady stream. Mix in poppy seeds, salt and pepper to taste.

LENTIL SALAD WITH CURRY VINAIGRETTE

Chilled food stuns taste buds and locks in aroma. This salad is an example of a dish that delivers full flavor only at room temperature, or slightly below. Allow it to stand in the cool part of the kitchen for an hour or so before serving.

> 1 pound lentils, washed and drained
> 6 cups cold water
> 1 large onion studded with 2 cloves
> 1 bay leaf
> Salt and pepper
> Curry Vinaigrette (recipe follows)
> 2 small carrots, cut in small dice
> 2 sweet red peppers, cut in small dice
> 1 green pepper, cut in small dice
> 1 medium red onion, cut in small dice
> 1/4 cup finely chopped fresh cilantro

1. Simmer lentils in water with onion, bay leaf and salt and pepper to taste until barely tender, 25-30 minutes. Drain, discard onion and bay leaf, toss lentils with 1/2 cup of the vinaigrette and let cool, stirring occasionally.
2. Toss with vegetables and remaining vinaigrette. Toss with cilantro.
Serves 6-8

Curry Vinaigrette

> 1 cup red wine vinegar
> 4 tablespoons sugar
> 1-2 teaspoons salt
> 1-2 teaspoons pepper
> 1 teaspoon cumin
> 2 teaspoons dry mustard
> 1 tablespoon curry powder
> 1/4 teaspoon ground cloves
> 1/4 teaspoon nutmeg
> 1/4 teaspoon cinnamon
> 2 tablespoons lime juice
> 1/2 cup honey
> 1/2-1 small jalapeno pepper, seeded
>   and minced
> 1 1/2 cups vegetable oil

Combine all ingredients except oil and beat well. Whisk in oil a little at a time.

TURKEY SALAD WITH CRANBERRY-APPLE RELISH AND ORANGE MAYONNAISE

The Pacific Northwest's native wild cranberry still can be found in certain spots behind the dunes along the coast. Commercial cranberry producers in Oregon and Washington, however, use stock that came from the East Coast.

Because most people eat cranberries at holiday time, here's a method of combining leftover turkey, a variation of the standard American cranberry relish and a zesty mayonnaise into a salad. (Try the salad as a sandwich filling.)

>　5 cups cubed cooked turkey meat
>　2 cups bite-size pieces blanched broccoli
>　1 purple onion, diced
>　4 stalks celery, sliced 1/4 inch thick
>　1/2 cup coarsely chopped fresh mint
>　　Salt and pepper
>　　Orange Mayonnaise (recipe follows)
>　2 cups Cranberry-Apple Relish (recipe
>　　on page 97)

Mix turkey, vegetables and mint. Salt and pepper to taste. Stir in Orange Mayonnaise to moisten. Fold in Cranberry-Apple Relish without overmixing, which causes colors to run.
Serves 6-8

Orange Mayonnaise

>　1 cup orange juice
>　　1-by-2-inch piece orange peel
>　2 eggs
>　1/4 cup rice wine vinegar
>　2 tablespoons lemon juice
>　　Salt and pepper
>　1 tablespoon orange zest
>　2 cups vegetable oil

1. Boil orange juice with peel, reducing to 1/4 cup. Discard peel and cool.
2. In blender or food processor, mix all ingredients except oil. With machine running, add oil in a thin, steady stream.

APPLE-CHICKEN SALAD WITH TOMATO CHUTNEY DRESSING

According to your preference, use Golden Delicious apples for sweetness or Granny Smiths for sourness in this main-course salad. Poaching the chicken properly is the key to an ideal salad. Overcooking renders it tough and dry.

>　3 whole chicken breasts
>　3 apples, peeled, cored and cut in
>　　1-inch cubes
>　3 stalks celery, sliced in 1/2-inch pieces
>　2 scallions, sliced thinly
>　　Salt and pepper
>　　Tomato Chutney Dressing
>　　　(recipe follows)

1. Gently poach chicken breasts in simmering water for 10 minutes. Turn off heat and let stand in hot water for 10 minutes. Drain and cool. Remove skin and bone, and cut into 3/4-inch cubes.
2. Mix chicken, apples, celery and scallions. Salt and pepper to taste. Mix with dressing.
Serves 6-8

Tomato Chutney Dressing

>　2 eggs
>　2 tablespoons raspberry vinegar
>　3 tablespoons lemon juice
>　1 tablespoon Dijon mustard
>　2 cups vegetable oil
>　1 cup Tomato-Hazelnut Chutney
>　　(recipe on page 96)
>　　Salt and pepper

In blender or food processor, mix eggs, vinegar, lemon juice and mustard until combined. With machine running, add oil in thin, steady stream. Fold in Tomato-Hazelnut Chutney. Salt and pepper to taste.

Asparagus
Salad with
Jicama and
Walnuts

Smoked
Salmon and
Potato Salad
with Creamy
Dill
Vinaigrette

ASPARAGUS SALAD WITH JICAMA AND WALNUTS

In the spring, when Washington's Yakima Valley produces some of the best asparagus on earth, aficionados invent many ways to take advantage of this prince of green vegetables. A plate of this salad and a chunk of bread constitute a light lunch. Don't make the salad in advance, however, since the dressing discolors the asparagus if they're in contact too long.

> 2 pounds asparagus
> 1/2 cup light soy sauce
> 1/2 cup sugar
> 1/2 cup rice wine vinegar
> 1/2 tablespoon minced fresh ginger
> 4 tablespoons walnut oil
> 2 cups walnuts, oven-toasted and
>   chopped coarsely
> 1 pound jicama, peeled and cut in
>   1-inch-thick strips
> 1/4 cup chopped cilantro

1. Snap off tough ends of asparagus. Peel stalks. Steam until just tender. (They should be still crisp.) Cut on diagonal in 1-inch pieces. Keep warm.
2. Meanwhile, combine soy sauce, sugar, vinegar, ginger and walnut oil in small saucepan. Cook over low heat until sugar dissolves. Remove from heat and add walnuts.
3. Combine asparagus and jicama and ladle on warm dressing. Toss with cilantro and serve.

Serves 4-6

SMOKED SALMON AND POTATO SALAD WITH CREAMY DILL VINAIGRETTE

Ample supplies of smoked salmon are available to Pacific Northwesterners. Here's one way to enjoy the buttery type from the cold-smoked process, also called lox- or nova-style. Serve this salad either to begin a large meal or as the centerpiece of a luncheon.

> 8 small red potatoes
>   Creamy Dill Vinaigrette
>   (recipe follows)
> 1/2 fennel bulb, cut in small dice
> 1/2 sweet red pepper, cut in small dice
> 1/2 green pepper, cut in small dice
> 1/2 red onion, cut in small dice
> 1/4 cup minced parsley
>   Salt and pepper
> 1 bunch watercress, stems removed
> 1 large head butter lettuce
> 4 ounces cold-smoked salmon, cut in
>   bite-size pieces
> 1/4 cup sour cream
> 8-12 croutons (see note)
> 1/4 cup fresh salmon roe

1. Boil unskinned potatoes in salted water until tender. Drain and cool enough to handle. Slice thinly. Toss with some of the vinaigrette to moisten. Toss again with fennel, red and green peppers, onion, half the parsley and more vinaigrette. Salt and pepper to taste. Refrigerate to chill slightly.
2. To serve, tear watercress and lettuce, toss with vinaigrette and divide among plates. Arrange potato mixture on greens, top with smoked salmon and sprinkle with remaining parsley.
3. Spread sour cream on croutons, top with salmon roe and serve with salad.

Serves 4-6

Creamy Dill Vinaigrette

> 1 egg
> 1 cup olive oil
> 2 teaspoons Dijon mustard
> 2 tablespoons white wine vinegar
> 1 tablespoon lemon juice
> 1 teaspoon sugar
>   Salt and pepper
> 1 tablespoon minced fresh dill

Beat egg in food processor or blender until just foamy. With machine running, add oil in a thin, steady stream. Briefly mix in remaining ingredients.

Note: *To make croutons, slice French or Italian bread, butter slices (or brush both sides with olive oil) and toast in a 325° F oven until lightly browned.*

SMOKED OYSTER SALAD WITH ORANGE-SOY DRESSING

Pacific Northwest smoked oysters aren't tiny little things that come in shallow cans. At their best, they're plump and moist, superb with a hoppy cold beer or a crisp, herbaceous local Semillon Blanc. In this recipe, grilled smoked oysters are combined with greens for a main-course luncheon salad. The greens shouldn't be too cold and the oysters shouldn't be too hot. Allow the greens to sit at room temperature for a half-hour before serving. Just warm the oysters on the grill; they don't have to be cooked.

> *1/2 pound snow peas, trimmed*
> *1 head butter lettuce, torn*
> *1 bunch spinach, stems removed
>   and torn*
> *2 heads Belgian endive, cut in
>   thin slices*
> *1 sweet red pepper, cut in thin slices
>   Orange-Soy Dressing (recipe follows)*
> *12 smoked oysters, warmed on the grill*

1. Blanch snow peas in boiling water for 30-40 seconds. Plunge immediately in cold water to cool and set color. Drain and pat dry with paper towels.
2. Toss vegetables with Orange-Soy Dressing. Divide among serving plates and arrange warm oysters on top.

Serves 4

Orange-Soy Dressing

> *Juice of 4 oranges*
> *1/2-inch slice of orange peel*
> *2 tablespoons light soy sauce*
> *1 teaspoon salt*
> *1/2 tablespoon sesame oil*
> *1 tablespoon lime juice*
> *1 teaspoon Dijon mustard*
> *1 teaspoon rice vinegar*
> *1/2 cup olive oil*
> *1 tablespoon minced cilantro*
> *1 small jalapeno pepper, seeded
>   and minced*
> *1/2 teaspoon orange zest*

1. Combine orange juice and orange peel and boil to reduce to 1/2 cup. Discard peel. Cool.
2. Combine orange juice with soy sauce, salt, sesame oil, lime juice, mustard and rice vinegar. Whisk in olive oil. Stir in cilantro, jalapeno pepper and orange zest.

SQUID SALAD

Tender squid are essential for this preparation. Use only fresh squid and don't overcook. You'll be rewarded with a salad that looks superb on a buffet table and brings out the delicate flavor of squid instead of overwhelming it, as frying does.

> *5 quarts boiling, lightly salted water*
> *3 pounds fresh squid, cleaned*
> *1/2 cup minced fresh dill*
> *3/4 cup chopped parsley*
> *1 1/2 cups chopped onion*
> *1/4 cup chopped fresh basil*
> *3 cloves garlic, minced
>   Salt and pepper (to taste)*
> *1 1/2 cups olive oil, extra-virgin if possible*
> *1/2 cup white wine vinegar
>   Zest of 1 lemon*
> *2 lemons, peeled, sliced thinly and
>   chopped*

1. Drop squid into boiling water, return to boil and cook until just done, 5-7 minutes. Drain, cool and cut into thin rings. Cut tentacles into bite-size pieces.
2. Mix remaining ingredients with squid. Place in glass or enamel bowl, cover with plastic wrap and refrigerate 12-24 hours before serving.

Serves 6-10

WILD RICE SALAD WITH SMOKED DUCK

In the shallow lakes and floodplains of the Coeur d'Alene, St. Maries and St. Joe river valleys of the Idaho Panhandle, wild rice is cultivated. There are only 1,200 acres, no more than a tiny patch compared to other North American wild-rice areas. And 800 of Idaho's acres are set aside for wild fowl. But the crop that does reach the market is prime long-grained rice of the "lakes" variety, the original type that is North America's only native grain.

Wild rice is not rice at all, but an aquatic grass. Nevertheless, its nutty flavor and nutritiousness make it increasingly popular. Here it's combined with firm Italian white rice, sweet pears and the gamy flavor of smoked duck to form a delicious, chewy main-course salad.

> 1 pound wild rice, preferably long-grain, rinsed and drained
> 4 tablespoons vegetable oil
> 1/2 pound Italian Arborio rice
>   Juice of 1/2 lemon
>   Salt and pepper
>   Honey Vinaigrette (recipe follows)
> 2 pears, peeled, cored and cut into medium dice
> 1 bunch spinach, stems removed
> 1 pound smoked duck breast, sliced thinly
> 1 bunch watercress, stems removed
> 1 tablespoon sesame seeds, toasted in dry skillet

1. Cook wild rice according to package directions, about 40 minutes. Drain and toss with 2 tablespoons of the vegetable oil.
2. Cook Arborio rice according to package directions, being careful not to overcook. (It should be firm when bitten, cooked just through.) Drain and toss with remaining 2 tablespoons of vegetable oil and lemon juice.
3. Combine rices while still warm, salt and pepper to taste and toss with 1 cup Honey Vinaigrette. Just before serving, add pears and toss with more Honey Vinaigrette.
4. To serve, line plates with spinach, spoon on rice mixture, fan duck slices along one side, garnish with watercress, drizzle more Honey Vinaigrette over and sprinkle with sesame seeds.

Serves 6

Honey Vinaigrette

> 1/2 cup raspberry vinegar
> 1/2 cup rice wine vinegar
> 1/2 tablespoon Dijon mustard
> 1/2 cup molasses
> 1/4 cup honey
> 3 tablespoons smooth peanut butter
>   Salt and pepper
> 1 cup vegetable oil

Mix all ingredients except vegetable oil in blender or food processor. With machine running, add oil in thin, steady stream.

BREAD AND ONION SALAD WITH PESTO VINAIGRETTE

Walla Walla Sweets are among those mild summer onion varieties (Maui, Texas and Vidalia are others) that have become as sought-after as designer jeans. The Walla Walla Valley, in the shadow of southeastern Washington's Blue Mountains, produces

asparagus, peas, wheat and many other crops. But the valley's reputation outside the Pacific Northwest rests on the juicy sweetness of its special onions. The seeds of the first Walla Walla Sweets arrived in the valley at the turn of the century in the pocket of a French soldier who had obtained them on the island of Corsica. Italian immigrant farmers in the valley took over from there, improving the onions with selective breeding and eventually spreading their fame.

Walla Walla Sweets are best eaten raw, so their character is not lost. This layered salad, which should be chilled overnight to blend flavors, is an example of how the onions lend distinction to recipes that can be made with any onion. Make it in the summer, when the onions and tomatoes are fresh, and serve it with barbecued meats, poultry or fish.

> Large loaf country-style French or
> Italian bread
> Olive oil
> 1 garlic clove, crushed lightly
> 4 tomatoes, peeled, seeded, quartered
> and sliced ¹/₂ inch thick
> 2 large Walla Walla Sweet onions, cut
> in half-circle slices ¹/₄ inch
> thick
> 3 cups fresh basil leaves, cut in ¹/₂-inch
> strips
> Salt and pepper
> Pesto Vinaigrette (recipe follows)

1. Slice away crust of bread. Slice loaf in half lengthwise and then in ³/₄-inch-thick slices crosswise. Brush with olive oil. Toast in 350° F oven until light brown. Rub warm toast with crushed garlic. Cool and cut into cubes.

2. Spread half the bread cubes in bottom of large straight-sided glass salad bowl. Spread with one-quarter of the tomato slices, then one-quarter of the onion slices, then one-quarter of the basil strips. Salt and pepper to taste. Drizzle with part of the Pesto Vinaigrette. Repeat layering with remainder of ingredients. Cover tightly and refrigerate overnight. Allow to come to room temperature before serving.

Serves 6-8

Pesto Vinaigrette

> 1 cup minced fresh basil
> 1 cup minced Italian parsley
> 2 cloves garlic, minced
> ¹/₂ cup red wine vinegar
> Salt and pepper
> 1 ¹/₂ cups extra-virgin olive oil

Mix herbs, garlic, vinegar and salt and pepper to taste. Whisk in olive oil.

THE CASCADES

In Search of Cascadian Treasures

The first one off on the hunt is Angelo Pellegrini. Midway in his ninth decade, he's as eager as he was 80 years ago when he strode the Tuscan hills of his native Italy, carrying then as he does now a bucket to receive his quarry.

His wife, Virginia, trails behind, her eye gathering in the mountains' autumn colors. Fanning out in the woods are two of the Pellegrinis' offspring, Angela and Brent. All are armed with knives.

It is October in the Cascade Mountains of Washington. In the logged-off area underneath the power lines, the sun still carries a hint of summer. In the forest's shade, where the Pellegrinis eye the ground, moss shines with melted frost.

It is time, once again, to hunt the Pellegrinis' favorite mushroom, *Boletus edulis*.

With luck, their knives will flash often this day, slicing through the creamy, bulbous stems of the mushroom known as the King. With luck, their buckets will fill to overflowing, as they do so often, and the midday lunch of sandwiches, fruit, cheese and homemade Cabernet Sauvignon will be enlivened with tales of where this mushroom was hidden and that mushroom was found.

On the other hand, perhaps the rains have not been

PASTA

41

sufficient. Or perhaps someone else has been in this place recently and Angelo will be forced to intone the bittersweet lament of the disappointed Italian mushroom hunter: *Ci sono bell'estati!*–others have been happily here ahead of us.

Precisely where the Pellegrinis are cannot be revealed. "Somewhere in the Cascades between Canada and Oregon," Angelo likes to say, when queried about the location of his many successful hunts, even as he dishes up heaping plates of boletes he has cooked for the delectation of his interrogators. Mushroom hunters are like that– at once generous and secretive.

But then novice Pacific Northwest mushroom hunters need not be led to these storied fungi. The region's forests and meadows abound with mushrooms, some 50 of which are edible and 20 considered choice.

To those of European heritage, boletes, morels and chanterelles are foremost. To those of Asian heritage, particularly Japanese, the snowy matsutake takes first prize. Not uncommon in the forests where the Pellegrinis hunt, in fact, is the sight of matsutake hunters calling out the location of boletes and other varieties for the benefit of fellow hunters as they plunge ahead in their single-minded quest.

Whatever the variety, wild mushrooms enhance cookery. Fresh or dried, they lend distinction to soups and sauces or stand on their own as accompaniments to everything from oysters to roast beef. Few mushrooms can be cultivated. The most common of those that can, *Agaricus bisporus*, the white "button" mushroom found in every supermarket, can be substituted in any recipe calling for wild mushrooms. But those who know only the button mushroom's flavor are missing a wealth of gustatory delight.

The Pellegrinis appreciate nearly all of the Pacific Northwest's mushrooms. Angelo, a professor emeritus of English at the University of Washington, is an authority on cooking. In his many books and articles, he has often written about wild mushrooms. Here are his simple directions for the basic mushroom sauté: "Heat equal parts of olive oil and butter, a generous tablespoon of each for a pound of mushrooms–more if one likes fat and has no fear of it. When it is hot, drop in two cloves of garlic coarsely chopped, a tablespoon of minced parsley and a teaspoon of minced pennyroyal [or, as he explains later, another herb such as oregano or what Italians know as nepitella]. When these begin to sizzle in the skillet–and remember not to let them brown or burn–add the mushrooms, stir briskly, sprinkle with salt and pepper, reduce the heat and let them cook slowly. That is all."

Many varieties of wild mushrooms are now widely available in Pacific Northwest markets. True mushroom hunters like to gather their own, however, for a mushroom hunt, like those for wild blackberries or huckleberries, or game animals, takes one into the mountains that make the Pacific Northwest so distinctive. From volcanic ranges like the Cascades long ago came the soil that nurtures so many of the region's crops. The mountains create the climatic zones that produce the region's astonishing variety of edibles. And their slopes hold the trees essential to the growth of wild mushrooms.

"I don't care if we find a single mushroom," Virginia Pellegrini says, pausing in the forest to blow the whistle with which she keeps in contact with her family. "I look forward to this every year. Aren't we lucky?"

The bounty of the Pacific Northwest is diverse as the elusive morels to be found on Cascadian slopes (see overleaf) and the mussels harvested from the coast, the latter shown at right with tagliolini and red peppers (recipe on page 48).

PASTA

PENNE WITH ASPARAGUS

Eastern Washington produces about 30 percent of the domestic commercial asparagus crop, principally in the Columbia Basin, the Yakima Valley and the Walla Walla area. Contrary to the thin-asparagus fad, most of this comes to market properly: thick and tender. Thin asparagus generally is tougher than thick, since woody fibers develop from the outside in after asparagus is picked; thin asparagus picked at the same time as fat, therefore, will contain more fibers than the thick spears. Because of the demand, however, some Washington growers are now sending a second, thin-spear crop to market in the autumn, when tired plants are unable to produce thick spears. This is inferior stuff. Better to serve the following dish in the spring.

For aesthetics, select either small or large penne to match the thickness of your asparagus choice.

Cooking asparagus is simple: Rinse spears under cold running water, paying particular attention to the heads, where grit might lurk. Snap off tough ends and reserve for soup. Peel stalks. Boil or steam until just tender.

>   2 cloves garlic, minced
>   2 shallots, minced
> $^{1}/_{2}$ cup olive oil
>   1 $^{1}/_{2}$ pounds tomatoes, peeled, seeded and
>   lightly crushed
>   1 $^{1}/_{2}$ pounds penne
>   1 pound asparagus, cooked and cut
>   diagonally into 2-inch pieces
>   1 cup grated Parmesan
>   2 eggs, beaten lightly
>   Salt and pepper

1. Sauté garlic and shallots in olive oil over medium-low heat until lightly colored. Add tomatoes and cook, stirring, for 8-10 minutes.
2. Cook penne according to package directions. Drain.
3. Mix asparagus and penne in warm bowl. Stir in Parmesan. Add eggs and toss to coat penne and asparagus. Toss with tomato sauce and salt and pepper to taste. Serve on warm plates with extra Parmesan.

Serves 4-6

MACCHERONI WITH FOUR CHEESES

"Macaroni and cheese" once was America's favorite pasta dish. Reborn with the Italian spelling and cheeses from the Pacific Northwest, such as gouda from Yakima, Washington, and cheddar from British Columbia or Oregon's Tillamook County, it is worthy of any table. Serve it for dinner as an accompaniment to, say, roasted chicken. Or accompany with a green salad and serve it as the main course of a lunch or supper.

>   6 tablespoons butter
>   4 $^{1}/_{2}$ tablespoons flour
>   3 cups milk
>   1 cup heavy cream
>   4 ounces goat cheese, crumbled
>   5 ounces extra-sharp cheddar, grated
>   Salt and pepper
>   1 pound maccheroni
>   4 ounces gouda, grated
>   2 ounces Parmesan, grated
>   1 tablespoon butter

1. Melt butter over medium-low heat in small, heavy saucepan. Stir in flour and cook 2 minutes, stirring constantly and taking care not to brown. Combine milk and cream and scald. Add milk and cream and bring to gentle boil while stirring. Lower heat and simmer 5 minutes.
2. Add goat cheese and cheddar and stir until melted. Remove from heat and salt and pepper to taste.
3. Meanwhile, cook maccheroni according to package directions. Drain and place in large, warm bowl. Add cheese sauce and stir in gouda and half the Parmesan. Transfer to buttered baking dish, sprinkle with remaining Parmesan and dot with final tablespoon of butter. Bake at 375°F until top is lightly browned, about 30 minutes.

Serves 4-6

Linguine with
Goat Cheese
and Greens

Fettuccine
with Scallops
and Fresh
Tomato Sauce

LINGUINE WITH GOAT CHEESE AND GREENS

Cheese is best made in small batches on the farm. It acquires distinctiveness that way, since the type of milk animals, their feed and the cheesemaker's ideas all come through in the cheese's flavor and texture. Fortunately, small producers of goat cheeses have sprung up throughout the Pacific Northwest.

The pancetta called for is unsmoked Italian-style bacon. Smoked bacon may be substituted. The greens may be a combination of any type, such as mustard, beet, turnip or spinach.

> 6 ounces pancetta, cut in small cubes
> 1 cup fresh bread crumbs
> 4 anchovy fillets
> 3 cloves garlic, minced
> 1 tablespoon minced Italian parsley
> 2 tablespoons olive oil
> 2 small leeks, white parts chopped finely
> 2 bunches greens, stems removed and cut in 1-inch strips
> 1 cup strong chicken stock (see Notes on Ingredients, page xi)
> 1 1/2 pounds linguine
> 1 pound goat cheese, crumbled

1. Sauté pancetta over medium heat until browned. Remove with slotted spoon and drain on paper towel. Place bread crumbs in same skillet and, stirring, sauté until browned. Remove and drain on paper towel.
2. Drain anchovies, rinse in warm water, pat dry and chop. Sauté with garlic and parsley in olive oil over medium heat, stirring, until garlic turns light brown. Add leeks and greens and sauté 5 minutes, stirring. Add chicken stock, raise heat and bring to boil. Lower heat and simmer 2-3 minutes.
3. Meanwhile, cook linguine according to package directions. Drain and add to skillet. Add pancetta.
4. To serve, divide pasta among plates, and sprinkle with goat cheese and bread crumbs. Serve hot.

Serves 6

FETTUCCINE WITH SCALLOPS AND FRESH TOMATO SAUCE

In late summer, when tomatoes reach their peak, prepare this as the main course for supper. Combining the hot pasta with the room-temperature sauce results in a just-warm dish, perfect for bringing out the best in the tomatoes.

Sauce

> 6 large very ripe tomatoes, cut in 1/2-inch cubes
> 2 cups fresh basil leaves, cut in 1/4-inch strips
> 3 cloves garlic, minced
> 1 1/4 cups olive oil, extra-virgin if possible
> Salt and pepper

Combine ingredients in glass bowl, cover and let stand in cool part of the kitchen for several hours. Stir occasionally.

> 2 cloves garlic, minced
> 1/4 cup olive oil
> 1 pound sea scallops, sliced horizontally
> Salt and pepper
> 1 tablespoon lemon juice
> 1 1/2 pounds fettuccine
> 2 tablespoons butter, softened
> 1/4 pound kasseri cheese, crumbled
> Basil leaves for garnish

1. Sauté garlic in olive oil over medium heat for 30 seconds, stirring. Add scallops, raise heat to medium-high and stir-fry until they are cooked through, 3-4 minutes. Salt and pepper, mix with lemon juice and remove from heat.
2. Meanwhile, cook fettuccine according to package directions. Drain and place in bowl and toss with butter. Toss again with tomato sauce.
3. Divide among serving plates, arrange scallops on top, sprinkle with kasseri cheese and garnish with basil leaves. Serve slightly warm.

Serves 4-6

SPAGHETTI ALLA MARCO POLO

Blessed with the Pacific Northwest's bountiful ingredients, good cooks constantly experiment, adapting recipes to include local items. Here's an example. Gary Flaten, chef at a Seattle restaurant/deli called Italia, years ago learned to cook an Italian pasta sauce that contained walnuts. With a plentiful supply of Oregon hazelnuts at his fingertips, he reasoned, why not substitute them for the walnuts? A few other adjustments, and presto!, he had a dish that quickly became a favorite among Italia patrons.

    1 *cup hazelnuts, toasted (see Notes on Ingredients, page xi) and chopped coarsely*
1 1/2 *cups pimiento-stuffed green olives, chopped coarsely*
    2 *tablespoons coarsely chopped sun-dried tomatoes*
    4 *cloves garlic, minced*
  3/4 *cup olive oil, preferably extra-virgin Salt and pepper*
1 1/2 *pounds spaghetti*
  1/2 *cup grated Parmesan*

1. Toss hazelnuts, olives, tomatoes and garlic with olive oil. Salt and pepper to taste.
2. Cook spaghetti according to package directions. Drain and toss in warm bowl with the sauce. Serve with grated Parmesan.

Serves 4

SPAGHETTI WITH CHANTERELLES

Apricot-colored, trumpet-shaped chanterelles have become so popular in the Pacific Northwest that they are now widely available in markets from early summer until late fall. Although the region has always had an abundance of these treasures, they seldom appeared at table outside the homes of avid mushroom hunters. Today, Pacific Northwest chanterelles are commercially harvested and shipped to Europe in such numbers that some people are alarmed about their possible depletion.

Here they're done Italian-style, in a cream sauce with pasta. The cheese called for is what Americans know as Romano. Italians call it Pecorino Romano, and it's worth seeking out the imported version in a good cheese shop.

    1 *pound chanterelles*
    1 *clove garlic, minced*
    1 *tablespoon minced Italian parsley*
  1/2 *tablespoon minced fresh thyme*
    4 *tablespoons butter*
    2 *tablespoons olive oil Salt and pepper*
  1/4 *cup dry white wine*
    2 *cups meat stock (see Notes on Ingredients, page xi)*
  1/2 *cup heavy cream*
1 1/2 *pounds spaghetti*
  1/2 *cup pine nuts, toasted in a dry skillet*
  1/2 *cup grated Pecorino Romano cheese*

1. Cut mushrooms into long slices about 1/4 inch thick.
2. Sauté garlic, parsley and thyme in butter and olive oil over medium-low heat for 1-2 minutes, without browning. Add mushrooms and salt and pepper to taste. Raise heat to medium-high and cook, stirring frequently, until the liquid has evaporated and mushrooms begin to brown. Add wine and cook until it has nearly evaporated. Add meat stock, bring to boil, turn heat to low and simmer until slightly thickened, about 5 minutes. Stir in cream and remove from heat.
3. Meanwhile, cook spaghetti according to package directions. Drain and toss in warm bowl with mushroom sauce. Sprinkle on pine nuts and Pecorino Romano and serve hot.

Serves 4-6

PAPPARDELLE WITH MORELS AND PEAS

Morel mushrooms and fresh peas arrive in Pacific Northwest markets at the same time. In restaurants, they're likely to turn up on the menu separately. Here they're combined to flavor the wide noodle called pappardelle to be served as a main or a first course.

> 2 cups shelled fresh peas
> 4 tablespoons butter
> 2 tablespoons water
> 6 ounces prosciutto, cubed
> 1 tablespoon olive oil
> 1 teaspoon red pepper flakes
> 1 shallot, minced
> 1 clove garlic, minced
> 1/4 cup minced Italian parsley
> 1 pound morels, cut in small pieces
>   Salt and pepper
> 2 eggs
> 1/2-1 cup heavy cream
> 1/3 cup grated Pecorino Romano cheese
> 1 1/2 pounds pappardelle

1. Simmer peas in butter and water, covered, over medium heat until just tender, about 5 minutes.
2. Sauté prosciutto in olive oil over medium heat until it begins to brown. Remove with slotted spoon and reserve. Add red pepper flakes, shallot, garlic and parsley and sauté 2 minutes without browning. Add mushrooms and stir-fry until moisture evaporates and they begin to brown, about 5 minutes. Add peas and butter and sauté 2 minutes. Salt and pepper to taste.
3. In large bowl, beat eggs with 1/2 cup cream and Pecorino Romano.
4. Meanwhile, cook pappardelle according to package directions. Drain and toss in bowl with egg mixture. Add mushroom mixture and prosciutto and toss. Add more cream if desired. Serve in warm bowls.

Serves 4-6

PAPPARDELLE WITH RABBIT AND BOLETES

Italians have difficulty understanding the American habit of eating pasta as a main course, but this dish is ideal as the center of a meal. If boletes are difficult to find, morels or chanterelles will substitute nicely.

> 1 rabbit, boned and cut in 1-inch pieces
>   (liver reserved)
> 1/4 cup olive oil
>   Salt and pepper
> 2 medium onions, chopped finely
> 1/2 cup diced pancetta
> 1/2 pound fresh boletus mushrooms
>   Needles of 1 sprig rosemary, minced
> 1/4 teaspoon allspice
> 1/4 teaspoon nutmeg
> 1 cup dry white wine
> 3 tablespoons tomato paste
> 3 cups chicken stock (see Notes on
>   Ingredients, page xi)
> 1 1/2 pounds pappardelle
>   Grated Parmesan

1. Sauté rabbit in olive oil over medium heat until lightly browned, about 15 minutes. Salt and pepper to taste.
2. Add onion and pancetta and sauté until golden. Chop the reserved liver and add to skillet. Stir-fry 2-3 minutes.
3. Add boletes and stir-fry about 5 minutes, until mushroom liquid evaporates. Add rosemary, allspice and nutmeg. Add wine and let it evaporate.
4. Combine tomato paste and chicken stock. Add to rabbit. Turn heat to low, cover and simmer 30 minutes, until rabbit is tender.
5. Meanwhile, cook pappardelle according to package directions. Drain and place in warm bowl. Toss with half the rabbit sauce and 1/4 cup Parmesan. Divide among plates, top with remaining sauce and serve. Pass extra Parmesan at the table.

Serves 4

Smoked
Shellfish,
Penne and
Roasted
Pepper Salad
with Tomato
Vinaigrette

Tagliolini
with Mussels

SMOKED SHELLFISH, PENNE AND ROASTED PEPPER SALAD WITH TOMATO VINAIGRETTE

North Americans have taken to pasta salads with an avidity that shocks Italians. Some of the preparations deserve their scorn. Others are sensational, and even Italians are eating them.

This combination offers tastes, colors and aromas to arouse any appetite. Serve it at room temperature so that the flavors emerge fully.

Oysters are the most readily available smoked shellfish. But many Pacific Northwesterners have smokers of their own, so they might include clams, mussels or shrimp in the dish.

 1 pound small penne
 ¹/₂ cup olive oil, preferably extra-virgin
  Salt and pepper
 1 pound smoked shellfish
 2 bulbs fennel, cut in thin strips
 2 sweet red peppers and 2 sweet
  yellow peppers, roasted and
  cut in strips (see Notes on
  Ingredients, page xi)
 1 bunch watercress, stems removed
 1 cup fresh basil leaves, chopped
  coarsely
 1 small Walla Walla Sweet onion,
  halved and cut in ¹/₄-inch slices
  Tomato Vinaigrette (recipe follows)

1. Cook penne according to package directions, drain in colander and rinse under cold water for a few seconds. Toss pasta with half the olive oil, then continue tossing while adding remaining oil little by little. Salt and pepper to taste.
2. When pasta has cooled, toss with remaining ingredients and then with Tomato Vinaigrette. Let stand 30 minutes and toss with more dressing, if needed.

Serves 4-6

Tomato Vinaigrette

 3 cloves garlic, minced
 ¹/₂ teaspoon red pepper flakes
 2 tablespoons olive oil
 2 large tomatoes, peeled, seeded and
  chopped coarsely
 1 cup coarsely chopped basil leaves
 ¹/₃ cup red wine vinegar
 2 teaspoons lemon juice
 1 cup olive oil, preferably extra-virgin
  Salt and pepper

1. Sauté garlic and red pepper flakes in the 2 tablespoons olive oil over medium-low heat 1-2 minutes without browning. Stir in tomatoes and basil and cook for 5 minutes, until tomatoes' juice has reduced by half. Cool in bowl.
2. Whisk in vinegar and lemon juice. Whisk in olive oil in a thin, steady stream. Salt and pepper to taste.

TAGLIOLINI WITH MUSSELS

How much pasta to serve? One-quarter pound per person seems adequate when the pasta is served as a first course, one-half pound when it's the main course. Proportions here are for a first course for six.

 2 pounds mussels, beards removed
 1 cup dry white wine
 2 shallots, chopped
 2 cloves garlic, minced
 1 tablespoon minced fresh chervil
 3 tablespoons olive oil
 1 fennel bulb, cut in thin strips
 2 sweet red peppers, roasted and cut in
  narrow strips (see Notes on
  Ingredients, page xi)
  Salt and pepper
 ¹/₂ pound butter, cut in 16 pieces
 1 ¹/₂ pounds tagliolini
  Chervil leaves for garnish

1. Steam mussels with wine and shallots in covered pot until they open. (Discard those that don't open.) Remove mussels from shells. Reserve. Strain liquid through double layer of wet cheesecloth into small saucepan. Reduce by boiling to 2 tablespoons.
2. Sauté garlic and chervil in olive oil over medium heat for 2 minutes. Add fennel, lower heat slightly and sauté until just limp. Add red peppers and heat through. Salt and pepper to taste. Add mussels, remove from heat and cover to keep warm.
3. Whisk 2 pieces of the butter into the wine reduction. Set over low heat and whisk in remaining butter 1 piece at a time. Salt and pepper to taste. Set saucepan into larger pan containing hot water to keep butter sauce warm.
4. Meanwhile, cook tagliolini according to package directions. Drain and place in warm bowl. Toss with three-quarters of the butter sauce. Add mussel-vegetable mixture and toss. Serve on warm plates with remaining butter sauce spooned over pasta. Garnish with chervil leaves.

Serves 6

CRAB RAVIOLI WITH LEMON-CAPER BUTTER

Only one type of crab will do for this dish: Dungeness, preferably brought live to the kitchen before being cooked. Make these ravioli about 2 inches square. Because the butter sauce is so rich, serve only two or three per person as a first course.

We give no pasta recipe here. Make sheets of pasta by hand or machine according to a standard recipe. Place dabs of the filling every three inches or so on a bottom sheet, spread a top sheet over and cut with a ravioli cutter or a sharp knife. In the latter case, moisten your fingers with water and pinch the ravioli edges shut.

The ravioli may be made several hours in advance and kept in the refrigerator under a floured towel.

¹/₄ cup fresh bread crumbs
5 tablespoons whipping cream
8 ounces cooked crabmeat
1 tablespoon butter, softened
2 egg yolks
 Salt
 Lemon-Caper Butter (recipe follows)

1. To make filling, soak bread crumbs in 2 tablespoons of the cream. Mix the bread crumbs, crab, butter and remaining cream. (If possible, use a food processor, but don't overmix.) Beat egg yolks and then beat into mixture. (Again, use processor, if possible.) Salt to taste.
2. To a large pot of boiling water add ravioli a few at a time, return to boil, lower heat and simmer until pasta is just tender, about 10 minutes. Remove with slotted spoon and drain.
3. Divide ravioli among warm serving plates. Spoon on warm Lemon-Caper Butter and serve immediately.

Serves 4-6

Lemon-Caper Butter

1 cup butter
2 tablespoons lemon juice
2 tablespoons capers, rinsed and
   squeezed dry
1 tablespoon minced parsley

Melt butter over lowest heat. Add other ingredients and warm until just heated through.

PENNE WITH SMOKED SALMON AND VODKA SAUCE

Smoked salmon comes in many forms and styles in the Pacific Northwest: kippered, hard-smoked and cold-smoked, to name three. Unfortunately, because there are no agreed standards, and brines and smoking methods vary from producer to producer, the only reliable guide to smoked salmon is taste. Any type will do in this dish, but cold-smoked (or nova-style) works best. Serve this as a first course or, with a green salad, as a light supper.

    5 tablespoons butter
    1/2 teaspoon red pepper flakes
    2/3 cup vodka
    1 cup tomato pulp (see Notes on
        Ingredients, page xii)
    1 cup heavy cream
    Salt
    1 pound penne
    4 ounces smoked salmon, cut in
        bite-size pieces
    3/4 cup grated Parmesan

1. Melt butter over medium heat in skillet large enough to hold the cooked pasta. Add red pepper flakes and sauté 30 seconds for aroma to burst. Standing as far away from skillet as possible, add vodka and ignite. Shake skillet until alcohol burns off and flames die. Add tomato pulp. Sauté 2 minutes. Add cream and simmer 5 minutes. Salt to taste, but lightly.
2. Meanwhile, cook penne according to package directions. Drain and add to skillet. Toss with sauce. Remove from heat and fold in smoked salmon and half the Parmesan. Serve with remaining Parmesan.

Serves 4-6

LINGUINE WITH SEAFOOD SAUCE

Squid, shrimp and scallops combine in this rich pasta dish that probably should be served in small portions as a first course.

    2 cloves garlic, minced
    1/4 cup minced shallots
    3 tablespoons olive oil
    1 pound squid, diced
    1/3 cup dry white wine
    1 cup chicken stock (see Notes on
        Ingredients, page xi)
    1 cup clam juice
    1 cup tomato pulp (see Notes on
        Ingredients, page xii)
    1 cup heavy cream
    2 tablespoons pesto
    1/3 pound cooked shrimp
    1/4 pound bay scallops
    Salt and pepper
    1 pound linguine
    4 tablespoons butter, softened

1. Sauté garlic and shallots in olive oil over medium-low heat for 3 minutes, stirring. Add squid, raise heat to medium and cook 3-4 minutes. Add wine and cook to evaporate. Add chicken stock and simmer 10 minutes.
2. Boil clam juice and tomato concassée in saucepan to reduce by half.
3. In separate saucepan, boil cream to reduce by one-quarter. Remove from heat and stir in pesto.
4. Combine squid mixture, tomato sauce and cream mixture. Simmer 5 minutes. Add shrimp and scallops and heat through. (Scallops will cook quickly.) Salt and pepper to taste.
5. Meanwhile, cook linguine according to package directions. Toss with butter in warm bowl. Toss again with sauce and serve.

Serves 4-6

LASAGNETTA WITH ASPARAGUS, ARTICHOKES AND PEAS

Luciano Bardinelli developed this "little" or "light" lasagna for his restaurant, Settebello, in Seattle. Bardinelli, born in Northern Italy, finds that the Pacific Northwest reminds him of home because of both the mountains and the quality of ingredients for his kitchen. His unsurpassed reputation in Seattle springs from his use of fresh local items in traditional Italian dishes. This pasta, served as an introduction to a main course at Settebello, is his homage to the asparagus and peas from Eastern Washington. For home cooks, it may be served either as a first or main course.

Fresh lasagne sheets are highly desirable here, in order to insure that the lasagnetta is light, but dried pasta may be substituted.

> 1 pound asparagus tips
> 4 medium artichoke bottoms
> 1 pound fresh peas
> 1/2 pound butter
> 1/2 pound flour
> 8 cups milk, scalded
>   Salt and pepper
>   Fresh lasagne sheets
> 1/3 cup grated Parmesan
> 2 tablespoons butter, cut in bits

1. Steam the asparagus tips until tender. Drain and reserve. Cook the artichoke bottoms in boiling water until tender. Drain and reserve. Steam the fresh peas until just tender. Puree all three together in a food mill or processor.

2. Melt butter over medium-low heat in heavy saucepan. Stir in flour and cook 3-4 minutes, stirring constantly and taking care not to brown. Add milk and bring to gentle boil while stirring. Lower heat and simmer 5 minutes. Remove from heat and stir in vegetable puree. Salt and pepper to taste.

3. Using enough fresh lasagne sheets to make four layers in a lasagne pan or an 11-by-13-inch baking dish, cook pasta: Place sheets one at a time in large pot of boiling, salted water. When pasta is just cooked but still firm in the middle, remove and immediately plunge into a bowl of ice water to cool. Remove and pat dry. (If using dried lasagne, proceed according to package directions.)

4. Form lasagnetta by layering bottom of buttered pan with pasta, spreading one-third of vegetable sauce over the pasta and sprinkling with Parmesan. Repeat until three layers of the sauce have been laid down. Cover with final pasta layer, tuck in edges, dot with butter bits and sprinkle on the remaining Parmesan. Bake at 375°F for 15-20 minutes, until browned and puffed. Let stand 5 minutes before serving.

Serves 6-8

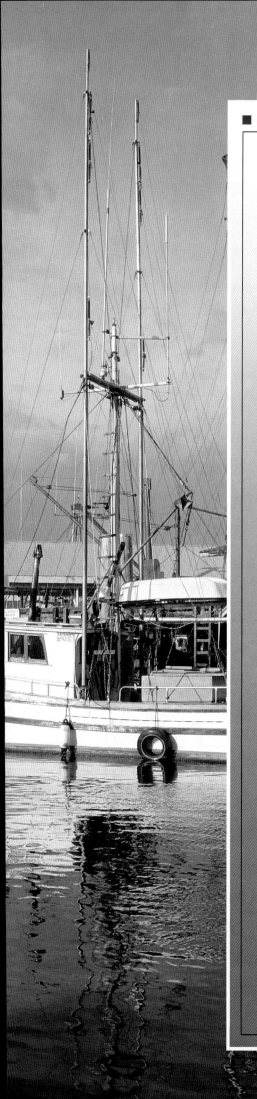

PORT ALBERNI

Home of Tall Trees and Fat Fish

Rain sweeps in gusts across Port Alberni, soaking the big pulp and paper mill, the two sawmills, the plywood plant and the fleet of fishing boats tied up on the waterfront.

"In the summer," Mike Carter says, "this place is dazzling. The sun shines and the mountains trap the heat so we're a lot warmer than, say, Seattle. But in the winter, we get rained on, that's for sure." Carter wears a suit and tie these days as manager of a waterside development of shops and restaurants called Harbour Quay. But he's a true Port Albernian, having worked, like so many of his 26,000 fellow citizens, at the mill and as a fisherman. Port Alberni, he'll tell you, is a workingman's town, a true Pacific Northwest coastal town where the trees grow tall and the fish grow fat.

"There's a lot of money in this place," Earl Kemps says, signaling for another schooner of beer in the pub at the Kingsway Hotel, near the waterfront. "Fishing and the mill pay pretty good. We're one of the strongest labor towns you can find anywhere. Hourly wages here are as high as anywhere else in British Columbia."

Kemps is a fisherman, working on a big purse seiner out of Vancouver over on the mainland during the spring,

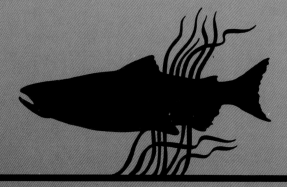

SEAFOOD

summer and fall, and relaxing during the winter. Evenings he can be found at the Kingsway, along with a roomful of other fishermen and mill hands, who play darts, shoot pool and spill beer on the tables, which are covered with yellow toweling for exactly that reason. Port Alberni is his hometown. He simply wouldn't have it any other way.

"Nice place to live," Kemps says. Indeed. Lying at the end of a 20-mile-long inlet that pokes deep into the heart of Vancouver Island, Port Alberni is the sort of place that first drew settlers to the Pacific Northwest. Men and women can make a good living here, and live well besides. "Five minutes in any direction," Mike Carter says, explaining his devotion to Port Alberni, "and I can be in the wilderness with a fishing rod in my hand."

Carter fishes nearby streams and lakes for rainbow, cutthroat and steelhead trout. When the big chinook salmon, locally called "springs," run up the inlet, he'll be out on a boat with a stout rod in his hands—stout because the salmon run large here, up to 60 or even 70 pounds. These giants are the stars of Port Alberni's commercial fishing business, but they have an impressive supporting cast.

From Port Alberni, fishing boats venture down the inlet, into Barkley Sound and out onto the Pacific in search of the full panoply of the Pacific Northwest's rich fishery. Fishing never really stops, but if there's a beginning, it's in March, when the herring season opens in Barkley Sound. That doesn't last long, four to six hours during one frenzied day, but the catch is valuable enough to draw nearly half the seiners of British Columbia. The herring are full of roe in March, and the Japanese pay dearly to obtain that roe.

After the herring, Port Alberni boats head out to sea for halibut. Then, in June, the salmon begin arriving back from their briny passage. That fishery lasts into September, and when it's over there are shrimp and prawns and clams—including the huge geoduck—to harvest. And Dungeness crabs, too, and sea urchin eggs for the Japanese and gooseneck barnacles for the Spanish. And, always, bottom fish such as lingcod and rockfish.

"A fisherman can work here year-round," Earl Kemps says, explaining his plans to buy his own boat and go into business for himself. "When it comes to West Coast fishing, you can't beat Port Alberni. We've got it all."

Port Alberni, on a secluded inlet deep inside British Columbia's Vancouver Island, is a point of departure for fishing fleets whose catch can itself become a point of departure for a piquant dish such as these crab cakes, flavored with mustard, lemon juice and peppers (recipe on page 71).

SEAFOOD

Poached
Salmon with
Red Pepper
and Basil
Sauces

Salmon
Baked in
Rock Salt
with Lemon-
Dill Butter

POACHED SALMON WITH RED PEPPER AND BASIL SAUCES

Poached salmon, a Pacific Northwest standard, can be served hot or cold and with many different sauces. In this instance, the salmon is served hot with two sauces that contrast in both flavor and color.

The Red Pepper Sauce, incidentally, is as versatile as tomato ketchup and a welcome alternative to it. Make a large batch and freeze, or preserve in hot-water bath according to standard procedures.

> Court bouillon for poaching (see Notes
>   on Ingredients, page xi)
> 6 salmon steaks
>   Red Pepper Sauce (recipe follows)
>   Basil Sauce (recipe follows)

Bring court bouillon to strong simmer in fish poacher or covered saucepan. Place salmon steaks in liquid and poach for 8-10 minutes at a gentle simmer until just done, when fish is opaque all the way through. Serve with Red Pepper and Basil sauces. Serves 6

Red Pepper Sauce

> 8 sweet red peppers, seeded and cut
>   into chunks
> 4 tablespoons olive oil
> 2 tablespoons balsamic vinegar
>   Salt and pepper

1. Sauté peppers in olive oil over medium heat a few chunks at a time, browning them lightly at the edges but not burning. When all peppers have been sautéed, return them to the skillet, cover, reduce heat to medium and cook until tender. Add balsamic vinegar just before peppers finish cooking.

2. Puree peppers in a food mill. Salt and pepper to taste. Warm slightly before serving with the poached salmon.

Basil Sauce

> 6 bunches fresh basil, stems removed
> 1/2 bunch fresh spinach, stems removed
> 5 sprigs parsley, stems removed
> 2 cups fish stock (see Notes on
>   Ingredients, page xi)
> 1/2 cup dry white wine
> 2 shallots, chopped
> 6 tablespoons butter
>   Salt and pepper

1. Blanch basil, spinach and parsley in boiling water for a few seconds. Drain. Cool under cold running water. Drain, squeeze dry and mince.
2. Bring fish stock, wine and shallots to boil and reduce to nearly 1 cup. Strain.
3. Combine chopped greens and reduced stock mixture. Simmer gently 5 minutes. Whisk in butter 1 tablespoon at a time. Salt and pepper to taste. Place saucepan in larger pan containing hot water to keep sauce warm until ready to serve.

SALMON BAKED IN ROCK SALT WITH LEMON-DILL BUTTER

Tina Bell recalls this method of cooking fish from her childhood in Trieste, Italy. The salmon emerges moist but not, if care is taken, unpleasantly salty. (Use a whole fish, including head and tail, so no skinless flesh is exposed to the salt.) The mustard lends a piquancy to the flavor, which is completed with the simple Lemon-Dill Butter.

> 6-pound salmon, cleaned and scaled,
>   with head and tail intact
>   Pepper
> 1 lemon, sliced thinly
> 1 tablespoon butter
> 1/4 cup Dijon mustard
> 3 cups rock salt
> 3 tablespoons olive oil
>   Lemon-Dill Butter (recipe follows)

1. Season cavity of salmon with pepper to taste. Stuff salmon with lemon and dots of butter. Close cavity carefully so that edges join and are not spread apart by stuffing. Spread mustard on both sides of fish.
2. Combine rock salt and olive oil in bowl. Line baking pan just large enough to hold salmon with heavy foil. Spread 1 cup of salt mixture on the foil. Place fish on salt bed. Gently press remaining salt mixture atop and around fish, enclosing it.
3. Bake at 450°F for 17 minutes. Remove salmon from salt, brush and pull skin off. Serve with dollop of Lemon-Dill Butter on each portion.

Serves 6-8

Lemon-Dill Butter

$^1/_2$ pound butter, softened
$^1/_3$ cup lemon juice
1 tablespoon minced fresh dill

Beat butter until shiny. Beat in lemon juice until absorbed. Beat in dill. (Best prepared in food processor.)

BRAISED SALMON WITH MEDITERRANEAN SAUCE

Fatty fish, like coho and chinook salmon, can withstand broiling or barbecuing without drying out. Less fatty fish benefit from other cooking methods, such as poaching or braising. For this recipe, with its aromatic, flavorful sauce, pink and chum salmon are ideal.

Pink and chum salmon are the least favored of the five Pacific species because of their relatively low fat content. Properly handled by fishermen and fishmongers, however, they can be extremely flavorful. Check them carefully in the market: Are their scales shiny and undamaged? Is their flesh firm and bright, with a translucent quality? Is the cavity free of blood and discoloration? Do they smell fresh and not too fishy? Any type of salmon should pass those tests, but with pink and chum, inspection is especially important.

4 tablespoons olive oil
1 celery stalk, cut in $^1/_4$-inch cubes
1 cup red onion cut in $^1/_4$-inch cubes
3 cloves garlic, minced
$^1/_4$ cup pine nuts
3 tablespoons capers, rinsed and drained
10 Kalamata olives, pitted and cut in sixths
2 tablespoons minced fresh oregano
2 cups tomato pulp (see Notes on Ingredients, page xii)
Salt and pepper
4 salmon steaks or fillets, $^3/_4$ inch thick
Flour for dredging
1 cup clam juice or fish stock (see Notes on Ingredients, page xi)
Lemon wedges for garnish

1. In a skillet large enough to hold the salmon pieces in one layer, heat half the olive oil and sauté the celery, onion and garlic over medium-low heat for 5 minutes. Stir in pine nuts, capers, olives, oregano and tomato pulp. Salt and pepper to taste. Cover and simmer 10 minutes.
2. Dredge salmon lightly in flour and sauté in another skillet in remaining olive oil over medium heat. Cook just 1 minute per side.
3. Transfer salmon to skillet containing vegetables and arrange pieces in one layer, heaping vegetables up and over the salmon. Pour in clam juice or fish stock and shake pan to distribute it evenly. Bring to boil, turn heat to low, cover skillet and simmer about 7 minutes, until salmon is just cooked through. Serve with lemon wedges.

Serves 4

SALMON HASH

Victor Pritzker, executive chef at Cascades restaurant in Portland, Oregon, was classically trained in French cooking. Long before that, however, he traveled as a boy with his parents and grew to love diner food. This colorful dish, one of the most popular at Cascades, is his homage to short-order cooking. "It's not sissy food," he says. "And don't be afraid of a very hot skillet for the potatoes."

> 4 medium Russet potatoes, peels on and
>   cut in 1-inch dice
> 1 cup vegetable oil
> 1 tablespoon chopped shallots
> 1 tablespoon chopped garlic
> 2 medium green peppers, cut in
>   1-inch dice
> 1 medium sweet red pepper, cut in
>   1-inch dice
> 1 medium sweet yellow pepper, cut in
>   1-inch dice
> ½ medium red onion, cut in
>   1-inch dice
> ½ medium yellow onion, cut in
>   1-inch dice
> 1 pound salmon, cut in ½-inch dice
>   Leaves of one stem fresh sage
>   Pinch rubbed sage
>   Pinch dry dill
> 2 pinches kosher salt
>   Black and white pepper to taste
> 2 tablespoons dry sherry

1. Soak potatoes for 10 minutes in two or three changes of cold water. Drain and pat dry with paper towels. Heat vegetable oil in heavy skillet until it's smoking. Fry potatoes, tossing and turning, 6-8 minutes, until they are nicely browned. Drain and reserve. Pour off all but ¼ cup of the oil, leaving brown bits from potatoes. Lower heat to medium.
2. In same skillet, sauté shallots and garlic 1-2 minutes, until they are lightly colored. Add peppers and onion and cook 2-3 minutes, until limp. Raise heat to high, add salmon and potatoes and toss several times, cooking just until salmon becomes opaque.
3. A few seconds before salmon is cooked, stir in herbs and salt, adding peppers to taste. Standing well away from skillet, pour in sherry and ignite it. Toss until flames are extinguished. Serve immediately.

Serves 4-6

GRILLED SALMON WITH HAZELNUT-LIME BUTTER

Until the venturesome new chefs of the Pacific Northwest loosed imaginations and educated taste buds a few years ago, it would have been unthinkable to serve a hazelnut butter with salmon. Grilling salmon was a summer ritual, for sure, but . . . hazelnuts? Well, no matter how it sounds, it's utterly delicious. In fact, you'd be wise to double the butter recipe and store the remainder in the refrigerator for a second go-around. Or, try the butter with poultry or another type of grilled or sautéed fish. Tightly covered to keep out alien flavors, the butter will keep for a week when chilled, even longer when frozen.

> ¼ pound butter, softened
> 1 tablespoon fresh lime juice
> 5 sprigs fresh cilantro, stemmed and
>   chopped
>   Salt and pepper
> ¼ cup minced toasted hazelnuts

Combine butter, lime juice, cilantro and salt and pepper to taste. Beat until silken. Beat in hazelnuts. Allow flavors to marry for 1 hour in refrigerator. Serve at room temperature.

> 2 pounds salmon fillets, skinned
> ¼ cup olive oil

Cut salmon into 6 pieces of equal thickness. Brush with olive oil and grill over hot coals about 3 minutes per side, or until just done. Serve with dollops of Hazelnut-Lime Butter.

Serves 6

Smoked
Salmon and
Scrambled
Eggs

Poached Red
Snapper with
Four-Pepper
Sauce

SMOKED SALMON AND SCRAMBLED EGGS

As have other Asian immigrants, the Chinese have had a strong culinary influence on the Pacific Northwest. Here's an example: an aromatic dish that can be quickly prepared for lunch, supper or even breakfast. Use any style of smoked salmon you wish, though we prefer nova-style in this recipe.

> *¹/₂ pound smoked salmon, sliced thinly and cut in ¹/₂-inch pieces*
> *6 eggs*
> *1 ¹/₂ cups chicken stock (see Notes on Ingredients, page xi)*
> *3 tablespoons light soy sauce*
> *1 ¹/₂ tablespoons minced fresh ginger*
> *1 scallion, chopped finely*
> *6 tablespoons vegetable oil*
> *1 tablespoon cornstarch*
> *3 tablespoons water*
> *1 ¹/₂ tablespoons red wine vinegar*

1. Beat smoked salmon, eggs, chicken stock and soy sauce together lightly.
2. Sauté ginger and scallion in 1 tablespoon of the vegetable oil over medium-high heat for 30 seconds. Remove and reserve.
3. Add remaining oil to skillet along with egg mixture. Cook, stirring slowly, for a few seconds. Add ginger and scallion while stirring. Cook about 2 minutes, scrambling eggs with fork.
4. Mix cornstarch with water, then stir paste into eggs to thicken. Stir in vinegar and serve.

Serves 4-6

POACHED RED SNAPPER WITH FOUR-PEPPER SAUCE

Fresh "red snapper" sold in the Pacific Northwest almost always is a species of rockfish and not a true snapper. Firm and pink-fleshed, red snapper fillets by any name are among the most popular choices in any fishmonger's case. Here, red snapper is poached in a bath of milk and fish stock and then served with a sauce containing a colorful mèlange of peppers. Yellow and red peppers have the same sweet flavor. Green pepper, however, contributes a different flavor, and the jalapeno provides bite.

> *2 cups fish stock*
> *2 cups milk*
> *2 pounds red snapper fillets*
> *Four-Pepper Sauce (recipe follows)*

1. In skillet or fish poacher, bring fish stock and milk to boil. Add snapper (add more milk and stock if needed to cover), cover, lower heat and poach at light simmer until snapper is opaque all the way through, about 10-15 minutes, depending on thickness.
2. Remove from heat and let fish stand in poaching liquid while sauce is prepared.
3. Ladle out ¹/₂ cup of the poaching liquid and boil in saucepan to reduce by half. Reserve for sauce.

Serves 4-6

Four-Pepper Sauce

> *¹/₃ small red pepper, seeds and ribs removed*
> *¹/₃ small yellow pepper, seeds and ribs removed*
> *¹/₃ small green pepper, seeds and ribs removed*
> *¹/₃ small jalapeno pepper, seeds and ribs removed*
> *¹/₂ cup tomato pulp (see Notes on Ingredients, page xii)*
> *1 tablespoon minced shallots*
> *4 tablespoons butter, softened Reserved poaching liquid*
> *1 cup heavy cream*
> *Salt and pepper*

Cut peppers in tiny cubes. Sauté peppers, tomato pulp and shallots in 2 tablespoons of the butter over medium heat for 3 minutes. Add reserved poaching liquid, raise heat and simmer briskly 4-5 minutes. Add cream and continue simmering until slightly thickened. Turn heat to low and whisk in remaining butter 1 tablespoon at a time. Salt and pepper to taste.

ROCKFISH IN BROTH WITH POLENTA

Some 50 species of rockfish inhabit the Pacific Northwest's salt waters. Among the most popular are yellowtail, widow and canary. But names mean little when it comes to rockfish because they vary so much from place to place. To confuse matters even more, red-hued rockfish often are called "red snapper," though they are not true snappers.

Whatever they're called, rockfish are tasty and relatively inexpensive. Their firm flesh is particularly suitable for soups and stews. Here, cooked in broth and served with the cornmeal mush Italians know as polenta, rockfish make a main-course soup with a Northern Italian accent. The soup is reminiscent of one Tina Bell knew in her hometown of Trieste, Italy, where a similar fish from the Adriatic is used.

> 6 pounds rockfish
> Flour for dredging
> Vegetable oil for sautéing
> 1 cup finely chopped onions
> 4 shallots, chopped
> 3/4 cup olive oil
> 3 cloves garlic, chopped
> Salt
> 2 cups fish stock (see Notes on Ingredients, page xi)
> 1 cup water
> 2 tablespoons tomato paste
> 1/4 cup red wine vinegar
> Salt and pepper
> Polenta (recipe follows)

1. Cut heads and tails off fish and reserve for fish stock. Cut fish into uniform pieces, about 3-inch squares.
2. Dredge fish pieces in flour, shake off excess and sauté in vegetable oil over medium heat until golden brown but not fully cooked. Drain on paper towels.
3. In saucepan, soup kettle or skillet large enough to hold fish in one layer, sauté onion and shallots over medium-high heat in olive oil until they begin to brown. Stir in garlic and cook 1 minute more.
4. Place fish in one layer over onions. Salt lightly.
5. In separate saucepan, blend fish stock, water, tomato paste and vinegar and bring to boil. Add to fish, bring to boil, lower heat and simmer, uncovered, 2 minutes. Turn over fish and continue simmering until fish is cooked and flakes with a fork. Transfer to warm platter and cover with foil to keep warm.
6. Boil broth in fish pan until reduced and slightly thickened. Salt and pepper to taste and add vinegar if desired.
7. To serve, spoon polenta into heated soup plate, place fish and onions on polenta and spoon broth over fish.

Serves 6-8

Polenta

> 2 quarts water
> 2 1/2 teaspoons salt
> 2 1/2 cups coarse-ground cornmeal (polenta, in Italian food stores)

1. Bring water and salt to boil in heavy saucepan. Stirring constantly, slowly add cornmeal in thin but steady stream.
2. Turn down heat to medium-low. Continue stirring, more or less constantly, 20-30 minutes, until polenta pulls away from sides of pan. (Polenta can be prepared in advance and kept warm in oven, or rewarmed. Cover tightly with foil.)

BRAISED ALBACORE WITH LEEKS AND TOMATOES

Michele Tennyson of Portland, Oregon, is a professional recipe developer with a particular expertise in seafood. Here, for example, is a dish she devised for the West Coast Fisheries Development Foundation to make use of the albacore tuna that Pacific Northwest fishermen increasingly

harvest during the summer. White-fleshed albacore usually come to market frozen, but when the fish are running close to shore, as they sometimes do, they frequently can be found fresh in good fish markets. In any event, freezing and handling methods have greatly improved recently, and high-quality frozen albacore are now available year-round.

> 1 ⅓ pounds skinless albacore, cut into
>   1-inch-thick steaks
> 2 teaspoons minced garlic
> 1 cup sliced leeks
> 2 tablespoons olive oil
> 2 medium carrots, cut in thin strips
> 16 ounces whole canned tomatoes,
>   drained and chopped coarsely
> 2 tablespoons chopped parsley
> ¼ teaspoon fennel seeds
> ½ bay leaf
> ¼ cup orange juice
>   Salt and pepper
> ½ teaspoon orange zest

1. Rinse albacore and pat dry with paper towels. In deep skillet or casserole, sauté garlic and leeks in olive oil over medium heat until just limp, about 5 minutes. Add carrots, tomatoes, 1 tablespoon of the parsley, fennel seeds, bay leaf and orange juice. Cover and simmer 5 minutes.
2. Place fish in a single layer atop tomato mixture. Cover and simmer about 8 minutes. (Fish should be opaque on the outside but slightly pink in the center.) Salt and pepper to taste. Serve with remaining parsley and orange zest as garnish.

Serves 4

STUFFED TROUT

Rainbow trout farming is big business in Idaho. The underground water source for the Snake River also provides trout farmers with ample supplies of fresh water at precisely the right temperature. Most of the US supply of pond-reared rainbow trout comes from Idaho, in fact. Many chefs say pond-reared trout are far superior to their wild cousins in flavor and texture because they are fed better.

At the Rock Creek restaurant in Twin Falls, Idaho, for example, manager Joe Knight swears by Idaho pond-reared trout. He favors a variety called Ruby Rainbow for its succulent deep-red flesh. Here's one method of preparation from the Rock Creek kitchen.

> ¼ teaspoon cayenne pepper
> 1 teaspoon dry mustard
> ½ teaspoon white pepper
> 1 teaspoon tarragon vinegar
> ¼ teaspoon minced parsley
> 2 cups heavy cream
> 8 egg yolks
> ½ pound butter, melted and cooled
>   slightly
> ½ cup chopped cooked shrimp
> 4 rainbow trout

1. Mix cayenne, mustard, white pepper, vinegar, parsley and cream in the top of a heavy boiler over barely simmering water and heat through. Beat in egg yolks one by one. Remove top of double boiler from heat and beat in butter in a thin, steady stream. Stir in shrimp. Cover and keep warm while cooking trout.
2. Remove bones from trout and open book-style. Place on greased broiler pan. Broil 2-4 inches from heat until flesh turns opaque all the way through, being careful not to overcook.
3. Top with warm sauce and serve.

Serves 4

Thresher
Shark on
Warm Greens
with Black
Bean
Vinaigrette

Poached
Lingcod with
Chardonnay
Sauce

THRESHER SHARK ON WARM GREENS WITH BLACK BEAN VINAIGRETTE

Shark has earned a spot on restaurant menus along all of America's coasts. In the Pacific Northwest, the shark of choice is the thresher, which has snowy-white flesh and a taste reminiscent of swordfish.

Sharks have no bones; their skeletons are composed of cartilage. The meat can give off an unpleasant ammonia odor if it's been poorly handled on the way to market. Soaking it in milk usually eliminates this problem. Low in fat, shark meat overcooks quickly and becomes tough, so extra care must be exercised. With that cautionary note in mind, a cook can readily substitute shark in most recipes calling for white-fleshed fish. Here it is prepared simply and served in a manner that will overcome hesitancy on the part of first-time shark eaters.

> 1 clove garlic, minced
> 1 tablespoon minced ginger
> 2 tablespoons peanut oil
> 1 bunch spinach, stems removed and cut in large pieces
> 1 bunch mustard greens, stems removed and cut in large pieces
> Salt
> 4 shark steaks
> Peanut oil for sautéing
> Black Bean Vinaigrette (recipe follows)

1. Prepare greens first. Sauté garlic and ginger in 2 tablespoons peanut oil over medium heat for 30 seconds, taking care not to burn. Add greens, stir to coat them, cover and steam 30-40 seconds. Salt to taste. Cover and keep warm.

2. In separate skillet, sauté shark steaks in peanut oil 2 at a time about 1 minute per side, removing from skillet immediately when steaks are opaque all the way through. Remove to warm plate, cover and keep warm while cooking remaining 2 steaks.

3. To serve, prepare bed of warm greens on each plate, place steak on each bed and spoon Black Bean Vinaigrette over.

Serves 4

Black Bean Vinaigrette

> 4 tablespoons light soy sauce
> 4 tablespoons sake
> 1 teaspoon Asian fish sauce
> 2 tablespoons rice vinegar
> 1 1/2 tablespoons sugar
> 1 teaspoon sesame oil
> 4-7 drops chili oil
> 1 tablespoon minced cilantro
> 1/2 cup peanut oil
> 1 teaspoon minced ginger
> 1 clove garlic, minced
> 1/4 cup black beans, soaked in water overnight and drained

Mix soy sauce, sake, fish sauce, rice vinegar, sugar, sesame and chili oils, cilantro and all but 2 tablespoons peanut oil until sugar is dissolved. Sauté ginger and garlic in remaining peanut oil over medium heat 30-40 seconds, taking care not to burn. Add black beans and soy sauce mixture, turn heat to low and stir-fry until heated through.

POACHED LINGCOD WITH CHARDONNAY SAUCE

The prizes of many Pacific Northwest wineries are their Chardonnays. One of the prizes of the Pacific is the lingcod, which is not actually a cod, but no matter. Marrying the two, as in this recipe, results in a memorable meal.

> 1 quart court bouillon (see Notes on Ingredients, page xi)
> 3 pounds lingcod fillets
> Chardonnay Sauce (recipe follows)

Smoked
Black Cod
with Ginger-
Soy Butter
and Jicama
Relish

Bring court bouillon to strong simmer in fish poacher or covered saucepan. Place lingcod in liquid and poach at a gentle simmer about 8 minutes until just done, when fish is opaque all the way through. Serve with Chardonnay Sauce.
Serves 6

Chardonnay Sauce

> 2 cups Chardonnay
> 1/4 cup shallots, minced
> 2 cups strong fish stock (see Notes on
>   Ingredients, page xi)
> 2 cups heavy cream
> 4 tablespoons butter
>   Salt and white pepper
>   Dash Tabasco
> 1 teaspoon lemon juice

1. Boil Chardonnay with shallots in saucepan until wine is reduced to about 1/4 cup.
2. Boil fish stock in separate saucepan to reduce to 1 cup. Add Chardonnay and shallot mixture. Stir in cream and boil until reduced to 1 1/4 cups.
3. Turn heat to low and whisk in butter, 1 tablespoon at a time. Salt and pepper to taste. Stir in Tabasco and lemon juice.

SMOKED BLACK COD WITH GINGER-SOY BUTTER AND JICAMA RELISH

Black cod, also known as sablefish, is found only in the Pacific. White-fleshed and rich in oil, black cod is widely enjoyed in the Pacific Northwest, both fresh and smoked.

Here's a method of smoking the fish easily at home while imparting to it the flavor of tea. Accompanying the smoked fish is a flavorful butter and a zippy fresh relish featuring crisp, juicy jicama.

Ginger-Soy Butter

> 1/4 pound butter, softened
> 1 teaspoon light soy sauce
> 2 teaspoons lime juice
> 1 teaspoon grated fresh ginger

Beat ingredients until silken.

Jicama Relish

> 1 cup diced jicama
> 1 cup tomato relish (see Notes on
>   Ingredients, page xii)
> 1 cup diced red onion
> 1 cup diced zucchini
> 1/2 cup chopped fresh cilantro
> 1 jalapeno pepper, seeded and minced
> 3 tablespoons lime juice
>   Salt and pepper to taste
> 2 tablespoons olive oil

Combine all ingredients except olive oil. Let stand 1 hour at room temperature. Drain and toss with oil. Chill slightly before serving.

Marinade

> 1/2 cup light soy sauce
>   Juice of 1 lemon
> 2 tablespoons sugar
> 2 cloves garlic, minced
> 4 black cod steaks, 3/4 inch thick
> 1 tablespoon sesame oil

Combine soy sauce, lemon juice, sugar and garlic and marinate black cod in mixture for 2 hours in refrigerator, turning 3 or 4 times. Wipe dry and brush with sesame oil before smoking.

Smoking Method

> 2 tablespoons black tea
> 2 tablespoons brown sugar
> 2 tablespoons raw white rice

Line wok, including cover, with 2 layers of heavy foil. Mix tea, sugar and rice and mound in bottom of wok. Place marinated black cod on oiled rack above mound. Turn heat under wok to medium-high. When rice mound begins to smoke, cover wok tightly and smoke fish 8 minutes. Serve with dollop of Ginger-Soy Butter on each portion and Jicama Relish.
Serves 4

RISOTTO WITH MUSSELS AND SAFFRON

Risotto, the wonderfully creamy Italian rice dish, is served as a first course in Italy. Here, it's offered as a main course. Accompany with a green salad and a dry white wine such as Chardonnay.

Short, plump Arborio rice from Italy is ideal for risotto since it can absorb the cooking liquid, retain the desired firmness in the center, maintain its shape and not turn sticky.

Steamed Mussels

> ¹/₂ cup dry white wine
> 2 tablespoons butter
> 3 cloves garlic, chopped
> 3 sprigs parsley
> 2 sprigs tarragon
> 3 pounds mussels, bearded

Simmer all ingredients except mussels for 2 minutes. Add mussels, cover pot and steam over high heat until mussels open, about 4 minutes. (Discard mussels that don't open.) Remove mussels from shells. Strain liquid in pot through double thickness of wet cheesecloth and reserve for risotto.

Risotto

> 2 tablespoons finely chopped onion
> 6 tablespoons butter
>   Strained stock from steamed mussels
>   Chicken stock (see Notes on
>   Ingredients, page xi)
> ¹/₂ teaspoon stem saffron
> ¹/₂ cup dry white wine
> 2 cups Arborio rice
>   Salt and pepper
>   Steamed mussels
> 2 tablespoons chopped parsley

1. Sauté onion in butter over medium-low heat in heavy saucepan until lightly colored but not browned, about 2 minutes.

2. Meanwhile, combine strained mussel stock and enough chicken stock to make 5 cups and heat to bare simmer. In separate small pan, boil saffron in ¹/₂ cup of the stock to dissolve. Set aside.

3. Raise heat under onion to medium, add wine and allow to evaporate. Add rice and cook 3-4 minutes, stirring to coat thoroughly.

4. A half cup at a time at first and less later, add simmering stock to rice, stirring constantly. When rice has nearly absorbed each portion of stock, add another. After 14-15 minutes, add saffron with its hot stock. Rice should be cooked to desired firmness in 18-20 minutes, and 4-5 cups of the stock will be needed. Remove from heat and salt and pepper to taste. Stir in mussels. Sprinkle with parsley and serve.

Serves 4

MUSSEL AND SAUSAGE STEW

Sounds odd, but the spicy sausage in this dish perfectly complements the sweet mussels. Serve it on a cold evening with a crusty bread to sop up the broth and a dry white wine such as a Semillon Blanc or even a red, like Pinot Noir. (If you're planning to serve a red, substitute it for the white wine in the recipe.)

> ¹/₂ teaspoon red pepper flakes
> ¹/₂ cup olive oil
> 2 small onions, chopped finely
> 1 pound hot Italian sausage, casings
>   removed
> ¹/₄ pound prosciutto, cut in ¹/₄-inch dice
> 4 large tomatoes, peeled, seeded and
>   chopped coarsely
> ¹/₄ cup minced Italian parsley
> ¹/₄ cup minced fresh basil
> 3 cloves garlic, minced
> ³/₄ cup dry white wine
> 4 pounds mussels, beards removed
>   Salt and pepper

Clams with
Sausage and
Chicken

Steamed
Clams with
Sake and
Ginger

1. Sauté red pepper flakes in olive oil over medium-low heat for a few seconds, add onion and sauté until soft but not browned, about 10 minutes. Add sausage, breaking it up with a fork, and cook until it changes color. Add prosciutto and cook 2 minutes. Add tomatoes, parsley, basil and garlic and simmer 5 minutes, stirring.
2. Raise heat to medium-high and add wine, allowing it to boil off. Add mussels, cover and steam until they just open. (Discard those that don't open.) Salt and pepper to taste and serve in soup plates.

Serves 4-6

CLAMS WITH SAUSAGE AND CHICKEN

The principal ingredients of this dish retain their distinctiveness while coming together in a spicy, aromatic broth that should be sopped up with crusty bread. As the British learned in the tropics, the best season for hot, spicy food might well be when it's hottest. A chilled, Pacific Northwest Sauvignon Blanc or cold beer or ale from one of the region's many microbreweries would be an ideal accompaniment.

> 2 medium onions, sliced thinly
> 3 tablespoons butter
> 3 tablespoons olive oil
> 3 cloves garlic, minced
> 1/2 pound chorizo sausage, cut into 1/2-inch slices
> 1/4 pound prosciutto or smoked ham, chopped finely
> 1 whole chicken breast, skinned, boned and cut in 1-inch pieces
> 1 1/2 cups tomato pulp (see Notes on Ingredients, page xii)
> 1/2 cup minced Italian parsley
> 1 tablespoon minced fresh oregano
> 1 small bay leaf
> 1 jalapeno pepper, seeded and minced
> 1/2 cup dry white wine
> 1 teaspoon paprika
> Salt and pepper to taste
> 3 pounds steamer clams

1. Sauté onion in butter and olive oil over medium heat in large skillet until lightly colored, 8-10 minutes. Add garlic and sauté 1-2 minutes. Stir in all other ingredients except clams. Simmer 10 minutes, stirring occasionally, to cook chicken and evaporate most of liquid.
2. Place clams on top of mixture, cover, raise heat to high and steam until clams open, 5-7 minutes. (Discard clams that don't open.) Serve in warm bowls.

Serves 4-6

STEAMED CLAMS WITH SAKE AND GINGER

The Manila clam is the most common steamer in the Pacific Northwest. The Asian accent of this recipe, then, is entirely appropriate. Serve the clams as a first course or, in larger amounts accompanied by an ample supply of good bread, as a main course. (The mirin called for in the recipe is a sweet rice cooking wine available in most supermarkets and Asian food stores.)

> 2-inch piece fresh ginger, peeled
> 1 cup sake
> 1/4 cup mirin
> 1 large clove garlic, minced
> 4 strands dried kelp (optional)
> 4 dozen steamer clams

1. In heavy pot with tight-fitting lid, bring all ingredients except clams to boil, lower heat and simmer 2 minutes. Remove ginger.
2. Add clams, cover and steam until shells open, about 5 minutes. (Discard clams that don't open.) Spoon clams into bowls, pour broth over them and serve.

Serves 4-6 as first course

**Grilled
Scallops and
Walla Walla
Sweet Onions
with Repulse
Bay Hotel
Butter**

GRILLED SCALLOPS AND WALLA WALLA SWEET ONIONS WITH REPULSE BAY HOTEL BUTTER

The succulence of scallops and Walla Walla Sweets is enhanced in this backyard-barbecue recipe by a flavored butter that Tina Bell and her children grew fond of while living in Hong Kong's Repulse Bay Hotel in the 1970s. There, the butter flavored escargots. The hotel's Swiss chef kindly shared the recipe with Bell. It's wonderful with meat and poultry, too. Freeze what's not needed here in small batches for later use.

30-36 *sea scallops*
   ¹/₂ cup olive oil, extra-virgin if possible
   2-3 large Walla Walla Sweet onions
      Salt and pepper
      Repulse Bay Hotel Butter (recipe follows)

1. Soak 12 wood skewers in water for one hour. Distribute scallops evenly on 6 of the skewers. Brush with olive oil and marinate in refrigerator 1 hour.
2. Peel and slice onions 1 inch thick. Divide slices and skewer.
3. Brush skewered onions with olive oil. Salt and pepper. Grill over hot coals in spot where heat is low for 5 minutes. Turn over, salt and pepper, and grill for 3 minutes.

4. Grill scallops over hot coals for 2 minutes. Turn, salt and pepper to taste, and grill another minute, until opaque all the way through.
5. Remove scallops and onions from heat, top with Repulse Bay Hotel Butter and serve.

Serves 6

Repulse Bay Hotel Butter

   1 small onion, chopped
      Cloves of 1 head garlic, peeled
   2 tablespoons olive oil
   ¹/₂ bunch watercress, stems removed
   ¹/₂ bunch parsley, stems removed
   4 sprigs fresh marjoram
   2 sprigs fresh tarragon
   5 fresh chives
   4 stems fresh thyme
   2 tablespoons lemon juice
   1 tablespoon Madeira
   1 teaspoon Worcestershire sauce
   1 tablespoon brandy
   1 tablespoon Dijon mustard
   4 anchovy fillets, chopped coarsely
   1 pound butter, softened
   2 egg yolks
      Salt and pepper

1. Sauté onion and garlic in olive oil over lowest heat, partly covered, for 20 minutes. Do not allow to color.
2. Blanch watercress and herbs in boiling water for 1 minute. Drain, refresh under cold water, drain again and pat dry in paper towels.
3. Place all ingredients except butter and egg yolks in food processor. Process to a smooth paste. Add butter and process until well combined. Add egg yolks and salt and pepper to taste. Process just until eggs have been well blended. Mixture should be glossy.

MOUSSELINE OF SCALLOPS AND COD SALAD WITH SORREL SAUCE

Though it sounds fussy, this dish goes together rather easily. It can be served as a main course with rice, or, in smaller portions, as a first course. For best results, chill the bowl and knife of the food processor in the freezer for 15 minutes before beginning. The cod and scallops also should be cold.

Mousseline Logs

1/2 pound true cod
1/2 pound sea scallops
2 egg whites
1 cup chilled heavy cream
1/2 teaspoon salt
  Two pinches pepper
  Pinch nutmeg

1. Chill food processor bowl and knife in freezer for 15 minutes before beginning. Puree cod and scallops in food processor. Add egg whites and process until well blended. With machine running, pour in 3/4 cup of the cream. Chill mixture. Beat in by hand as much of the remaining cream as the mixture will absorb without becoming runny. Beat in salt, pepper and nutmeg. Place mousseline in pastry bag fitted with a tip wide enough to produce a log about 1 1/2 inches in diameter.
2. To form logs, butter the bottom two-thirds of 10-inch lengths of plastic wrap. Pipe out logs about 4 inches long onto the buttered areas. Wrap the bottom of the buttered area over each log and roll up, using the unbuttered border to seal the package. Twirl ends to seal and tie with string.
3. Bring pot of water to simmer, gently slide in logs and poach 5 minutes. Cool, unwrap and cut logs into 1/2-inch-thick diagonal slices.

Serves 6-8

Sorrel Sauce

1/4 cup minced shallots
3 tablespoons butter
10 sorrel leaves, stems removed and cut into thirds
1/2 cup fish stock (see Notes on Ingredients, page xi)
1 cup heavy cream
  Salt and pepper
1 tablespoon balsamic vinegar

1. Sauté shallots in butter over medium heat until soft but not browned. Add sorrel and sauté 2 minutes. Add fish stock and boil to reduce to 1/3 cup liquid.
2. Add cream and simmer 5 minutes, until slightly thickened. Puree in food processor or blender. Salt and pepper to taste. Add balsamic vinegar and mix briefly to blend. Serve warm.

Assembly

3 avocados, peeled, pitted and sliced 1/2 inch thick lengthwise
2 papayas, peeled, seeded and sliced 1/2 inch thick lengthwise
  Mousseline slices
6 sprigs watercress

Alternate avocado and papaya slices in fan shape on 6 plates. Arrange mousseline slices in overlap pattern at base of fan. Garnish with watercress and spoon on warm Sorrel Sauce.

SCALLOPS AND SHRIMP IN SAFFRON-TOMATO SAUCE

In the late summer, when fresh tomatoes and local scallops and shrimp are plentiful, this dish goes together beautifully. Among its virtues are appearance (rosy gold) and, above all, flavor. Serve with steamed rice and a salad of crisp greens.

> 1 pound scallops
> 1 pound shrimp
> 4 cups fish stock (see Notes on
>   Ingredients, page xi)
> 1/2 cup white wine
> 1 small onion, chopped finely
> 1/2 small carrot, chopped finely
> 2 tablespoons minced parsley
> 1 tablespoon minced fresh thyme
> 3 tablespoons butter
> 3 tablespoons flour
>   Heavy cream
>   Salt and pepper
> 1/2 teaspoon stem saffron
> 1 1/2 cups tomato pulp (see Notes on
>   Ingredients, page xii)
> 1 cup fresh bread crumbs
> 1/3 cup finely chopped parsley
> 4 tablespoons butter, melted

1. Poach scallops and shrimp in simmering fish stock until just done, about 2 minutes, depending on their size. Remove with slotted spoon and keep warm.
2. Add wine to fish stock and boil 5 minutes. Strain through wet cheesecloth. Boil to reduce to 3 cups.
3. Meanwhile, in large skillet, sauté onion, carrot, parsley and thyme in the 3 tablespoons butter over medium-low heat until vegetables are soft, about 5 minutes. Stir in flour and cook, stirring, until lightly colored, about 5 minutes. (Take care not to burn.)
4. Combine cream and fish stock and heat to simmer. Stir mixture into sautéed vegetable mixture, bring to boil, lower heat and simmer briskly to reduce to 2-1/2 cups. Salt and pepper to taste. Strain through a fine sieve.
5. Stir saffron and tomato pulp into sauce. Add scallops and shrimp. Pour mixture into a shallow baking or gratin dish. Mix bread crumbs, chopped parsley and melted butter. Spoon over seafood. Broil 4 inches from heat until golden brown and serve.

Serves 4-6

HALIBUT SALAD

As a luncheon dish, or a starter for a more elaborate meal, this salad pleases the eye as well as the palate. The snowy halibut gleams in its bath of dressing, providing a backdrop for the vegetables' color. As always with seafood, be careful not to overcook the halibut, causing it to lose flavor and moistness.

> 2 tablespoons sherry vinegar
>   Juice of 2 limes
>   Tabasco to taste
> 1 1/4 cup olive oil
>   Salt and pepper to taste
> 2 pounds 1-inch-thick halibut steaks
> 2 tablespoons minced fresh cilantro
> 1 tablespoon minced fresh chives
> 1 tablespoon minced fresh basil
> 1/2 cup sun-dried tomatoes, cut in thin
>   strips
> 1/3 cup pitted and halved Kalamata olives
> 1/2 cup thinly sliced red onion
> 1/2 cup pine nuts, toasted in a dry skillet

1. Combine vinegar, lime juice, Tabasco, olive oil and salt and pepper. In a non-corrodible baking pan or dish, spread 3-4 tablespoons of the dressing and top it with the halibut in one layer. Pour over 1/2 cup of the dressing and marinate the halibut 1 hour in a cool part of the kitchen.
2. Bake halibut in marinade at 400°F for about 15 minutes, until steaks are just opaque clear through. Cool. Remove bones and skin and cut into large cubes.

3. Combine herbs with remaining dressing. Toss halibut with dressing, sundried tomatoes, olives and onion. Serve on chilled plates of lettuce with sprinkles of pine nuts.

Serves 4-6

GEODUCK WITH LAMINARIA AND PICKLED BLACKBERRIES

The largest clam in the world grows in great numbers only in Puget Sound and some of British Columbia's inland waters. Called "GOOEY-duck," this monster has been known to grow to 13 pounds, though most sold commercially weigh about two to three pounds.

Although imposing in size, geoducks are mild in flavor; most harvested commercially wind up in canned clam chowder. Both neck (siphon) and breast meat are eaten. The neck meat is crisper, like abalone. Care must be taken in cooking or the meat will toughen.

To clean a geoduck's neck, as for this recipe, drop the clam in boiling water for about 10 seconds. Using a small, sharp knife, remove the clam from its shell and pare away the viscera. Peel the skin away. Wash the meat, then slit the neck lengthwise and wash away any grit.

This inspired recipe was devised by Ron Cherry, a chef at Sooke Harbor House on Vancouver Island. Sooke Harbor House, a lovely little inn a half-hour's drive west of Victoria, looks out at the sea from atop a spectacular bluff. Equally dazzling is its cuisine, which is based on what can be grown and harvested locally. Laminaria, for instance, is a seaweed that is plucked from the shore. For those unlucky enough not to have laminaria in their backyards, it's widely available, fresh or dried, in Japanese markets, where it's called *kombu*. (Alaria, another seaweed, may be substituted. The Japanese call it *wakame*.)

Although this dish sounds difficult, it's quite easy to prepare, once the ingredients are obtained. And the symphony of colors and flavors it presents makes the effort worthwhile.

> 2 ounces laminaria seaweed, fresh or dried
> 2-3 tablespoons sesame oil
> 1 pound geoduck neck, peeled, cleaned and sliced $^1/_{16}$-inch thick
> $^1/_2$ cup dry white wine
> $^1/_2$ cup fish stock (see Notes on Ingredients, page xi)
> 4 tablespoons blackberry vinegar
> 4 tablespoons unsalted butter, softened
> 16-24 pickled blackberries (recipe follows)
> 3 teaspoons blackberry juice

1. Soak fresh laminaria in lukewarm water 5-10 minutes. (If using dried, soak 40-60 minutes.) Drain.
2. Heat sesame oil in heavy skillet until smoking. Cook geoduck quickly, 15-30 seconds, being careful not to overcook and toughen. Add seaweed and toss until warmed through. Remove to warm plate and keep warm while preparing sauce.
3. Deglaze skillet with wine, boiling until nearly gone. Add stock and vinegar and boil to reduce to 4-5 tablespoons. Remove from heat and whisk in butter.
4. To serve, divide geoduck and seaweed among warm plates and spoon sauce in ring around geoduck. Garnish with pickled blackberries. Dribble line of blackberry juice in middle of sauce ring and decorate by pulling fork crosswise through sauce.

Serves 4

Pickled Blackberries

> 2$^1/_2$ pounds fresh blackberries
> Cider vinegar
> 3 tablespoons sugar

Place blackberries in noncorrodible pot. Cover with vinegar. Stir in sugar. Bring to boil. Remove from heat and place in covered jars. Refrigerate at least 24 hours.

Pancakes
with
Dungeness
Crab and
Anchovy
Sauce

PANCAKES WITH DUNGENESS CRAB AND ANCHOVY SAUCE

America's new confidence in its own cooking permits such brazenness as calling pancakes pancakes, rather than crêpes. Nonetheless, these pancakes are recognizably French and the anchovy sauce owes a debt to the Mediterranean. The Dungeness crab, however, is gloriously Pacific Northwestern.

This is an excellent luncheon dish.

> 1 pound morels or domestic mushrooms, sliced thinly
> 5 tablespoons butter
> 3 shallots, peeled and minced
> 1/4 cup finely chopped scallion
> 1 cup tomato pulp (see Notes on Ingredients, page xii)
> 1 tablespoon minced fresh chervil
> 1 pound cooked Dungeness crabmeat
> 1/4 cup dry sherry
> Salt and pepper
> 12 5-inch pancakes (recipe follows)
> Anchovy Sauce (recipe follows)
> 1/3 cup capers, rinsed, drained and dried
> 12 lemon wedges
> 6 sprigs fresh chervil

1. Sauté mushrooms in 2 tablespoons of the butter over medium-high heat, stirring, until moisture has evaporated and they begin to brown. Remove from skillet and reserve.
2. Sauté shallots and scallions in remaining butter over medium heat, stirring, for 5 minutes without browning. Add tomato concassée and chervil and cook, stirring gently, for 2 minutes. Add crab, toss gently and cook until heated through, about 2 minutes. Add cooked mushrooms, raise heat to medium-high, add sherry and boil 1 minute. Remove from heat and salt and pepper to taste.
3. To serve, place a pancake on a heated plate, cover with crab mixture, top with second pancake, spoon on warm Anchovy Sauce and sprinkle with capers. Garnish with lemon wedges and chervil.

Serves 6

Pancakes

> 4 eggs
> 1 cup milk
> 1 1/4 cups flour
> 1/4 cup water
> 1/2 teaspoon salt
> 3 tablespoons butter, melted and cooled
> 2 tablespoons melted butter mixed with 2 tablespoons vegetable oil

Mix all ingredients except butter in blender or food processor. Stir in the melted butter. (Thin batter with milk, if necessary, to consistency of heavy cream.) Brush small skillet with some of the butter-oil mixture and place over medium-high heat. When skillet is hot, spoon in about 3 tablespoons batter and swirl quickly to coat skillet. Fry until light gold, about 1 minute, flip and fry 30 seconds more. Cool on rack. (Stack between sheets of waxed paper, cover with plastic wrap and freeze or chill if not using immediately.) Warm in low oven before preparing above recipe.

Anchovy Sauce

> 10 anchovy fillets
> 3/4 cup clarified butter (see note)
> Pepper

1. Drain oil from anchovies, rinse them briefly in warm water, pat dry with paper towel and chop coarsely.
2. Heat butter in small pan, add anchovies and mash with back of wooden spoon. Add pepper to taste. Serve warm.

Note: To clarify, melt butter over lowest heat in small saucepan. Carefully pour off melted butter, leaving milk solids behind.

DUNGENESS CRAB CAKES

The popularity of these crab cakes has made them the signature entrée at Cafe Sport, near Seattle's Pike Place Market. Chef Tom Douglas's creation doesn't overwhelm the sweetness of the Pacific Northwest's superb crab but heightens it by playing the sweetness off against the piquancy of the other flavors.

Douglas finds that commercial white bread, crusts removed, makes the ideal crumbs for the cakes.

> 1 egg
> 1 tablespoon yellow mustard
> 2 teaspoons lemon juice
> 2 teaspoons red wine vinegar
> 3 shakes Tabasco
> Dash Worcestershire sauce
> 1/2 cup vegetable oil
> 1/4 cup olive oil
> 1 pound cooked Dungeness crabmeat
> 2 tablespoons minced parsley
> 1/4 teaspoon pepper
> 1/2 small sweet red pepper, chopped finely
> 1/2 small green pepper, chopped finely
> 1/4 cup finely chopped onion
> 4-6 cups soft fresh bread crumbs
> Clarified butter for sautéing (see note)

1. Mix egg, mustard, lemon juice, vinegar, Tabasco and Worcestershire in blender or food processor. With machine running, add oils in a thin, steady stream.
2. Squeeze excess liquid from crabmeat. Mix with mayonnaise from Step 1 and all other ingredients except bread crumbs. Mix in about half the bread crumbs, until mixture feels pasty.
3. Roll mixture into 3-inch balls. Roll balls in remaining crumbs and flatten into hockey-puck shapes. Sauté in small amount of clarified butter until golden brown on both sides.

Serves 4-6

Note: To clarify, melt butter over lowest heat in small saucepan. Carefully pour off melted butter, leaving milk solids behind.

PRAWNS WITH GINGER, LIME AND CILANTRO CREAM

Patrons of a recent Taste of Vancouver festival voted this the best seafood dish, which was no surprise to regulars at Cherrystone Cove, in the city's Gastown area. They know that the Cove's owner-chef, Mark Potovsky, who devised the dish, is one of the hottest young cooks in British Columbia. Potovsky specializes in local ingredients, such as prawns, with an Asian touch.

The mirin called for is a sweet rice cooking wine available in most supermarkets and Asian food stores. Pickled young ginger is also available in Asian markets.

> 2 tablespoons mirin
> 1 teaspoon minced pickled young ginger
> 1/2 teaspoon minced garlic
> 1/2 teaspoon minced shallot
> 15-20 leaves fresh cilantro, chopped finely
> Juice of 1/2 lime
> 8 tablespoons whipping cream
> 1 Serrano pepper, chopped finely
> Olive oil
> 16-24 prawns (depending on size), peeled and deveined

1. Combine mirin, ginger, garlic, shallot, cilantro and lime juice in saucepan. Boil to reduce by half. Add cream and pepper and boil to reduce by half.
2. Meanwhile, heat olive oil in skillet until very hot. Fry prawns about 30 seconds per side, until just cooked through. Serve with warm sauce.

Serves 4

YAKIMA VALLEY

Vineyard of the Northwest

From the porch of Staton Hills' beautiful winery on a hillside just south of the city of Yakima, the wonders of Washington's Yakima Valley reveal themselves to a roving eye. The dry Rattlesnake Hills jut up to the north. The river runs among cottonwoods on the valley floor. Here, there and everywhere is evidence that this valley merits its reputation as one of the world's great agricultural areas.

World-class hops are grown here, most of the US supply. Likewise spearmint and peppermint. Beef cattle abound, especially in the upper valley north of the Rattlesnake Hills. A large portion of the nation's asparagus comes from the valley's southern reaches. And the orchards, so striking in their greenery against the stark earth tones of the unirrigated hillsides, have earned the Yakima Valley the appellation Fruit Bowl of the Nation. Yakima County boasts more fruit trees than any other county in the country. Apples, pears, cherries, plums, peaches and apricots grow here. And vineyards produce prodigious amounts of juice grapes.

MEAT & POULTRY

All of this, however, is being overshadowed by a single product that has gripped consumer attention: wine. Like the great agricultural valleys of Europe, the Yakima Valley seems destined to be known worldwide not for the cornucopia it is but solely for its wines.

That's fine with Rob Stuart, the 33-year-old winemaker at Staton Hills. He surveys the flowers and lawns in front of the winery, the elaborately trellised vineyards spilling neatly down the nearby hillsides, and talks proudly about the achievements of Pacific Northwest winemaking.

It is a remarkable story. Wine grapes had been cultivated for a century or more in the region, but they were local varieties, capable only of producing rough, sweet wines of no distinction. The Pacific Northwest's premium-wine business is barely two decades old, and its thrust onto the world stage began only in the mid-1980s. Yet the state of Washington now ranks second only to California in production of premium wines, Oregon produces international prize-winning wines, British Columbia's Okanagan Valley shelters a dozen fast-growing wineries and even Idaho wine labels are seen in Manhattan wine shops.

Most experts said it couldn't happen. The Pacific Northwest was too damp, too cold, to grow the *Vitis vinifera* grapes that produce all the world's great wines. They were wrong. They didn't understand the region's climate—how the mountain ranges, ocean air, cloudless desert skies and long summer days create countless microclimates that are ideal for *Vitis vinifera*, just as they are for so many other crops.

Stuart is aware of the skepticism. He has even shared it. Early on, Pacific Northwest growers and winemakers earned what little reputation they had with white wines, principally fruity Rieslings. Drier whites, like Chardonnay and Sauvignon Blanc, followed. Fine, skeptics conceded, decent white wines can come out of the region. But never reds.

"When I came here in 1985, that was my impression, too," Stuart says. "The reds were too oaky or overripe, which means the winemakers were masking something.

Since then, a lot of new vineyards have been installed, and I've seen a change. I think in the last two or three years, Northwest reds have evolved to the point where we're making world-class wines."

Indeed, experts who have studied the Pacific Northwest closely suggest that red wines will eventually outshine the whites. For now, Pacific Northwest winemakers continue their research and development and look outward to marketing challenges. Until recently, most wine produced here was also consumed here. Now grape production threatens to overwhelm the wineries, and domestic and foreign markets must be opened.

The marketing obstacle is California, or, more specifically, the California styles Americans associate with the way wines *should* taste. "We have a Northwest palate," Stuart says. "We like more acid, wines that are clean and crisp. But we've faced the fact that if we are going to sell outside the Northwest, we need to lower our acids.

"We Northwesterners say of California wines that they are flat and flabby and overripe, with not enough fruit. Californians say that our wines are green, underripe."

Yet such conflicts are music to winelovers' ears. From different opinions spring different wines, and the consumer benefits. Stuart, for instance, aspires to make a world-class champagne.

"That's why I came here," he says. "Champagne is what I think Staton Hills will someday be known for best. My objective is to make French-style champagne—less fruity and more complex than California champagnes. We'll do it, too. We Northwesterners can make wines that will be unrivaled in the world. Because we have the grapes to do it."

Washington state's eastern half has been a land of ranches and farmsteads since its glory as America's last frontier in the late 19th century. Now, the fertile soil along waterways such as the Yakima River (see overleaf) is nourishing some of the finest wine grapes in the world. Both past and present are represented in this setting of braised ham with cranberry sauce (recipe on page 76), complemented by a Washington wine.

74

MEAT & POULTRY

**Fruit and
Ham Torte**

**Braised Ham
with
Cranberry
Sauce**

FRUIT AND HAM TORTE

This is a dish for winter, when much of the Pacific Northwest is bathed in rain and gloom, and a blaze in the fireplace is more necessity than luxury. Serve it warm or at room temperature for lunch, dinner or as part of a holiday buffet. Accompany with a selection of mustards.

Brioche Dough

¹/₂ tablespoon dry yeast
   Pinch sugar
2 tablespoons medium-hot water
2 eggs
2 tablespoons milk
1³/₄ cups flour
1 teaspoon salt
6 tablespoons chilled unsalted butter,
   cut into bits

1. Dissolve yeast and sugar in water. Beat eggs and milk into yeast mixture. Stir in flour and salt. Knead on lightly floured surface into soft dough. Let rest 10 minutes. Knead butter into dough. Let rest 10 minutes. Knead 1 minute. Let rise about 40 minutes in bowl covered with plastic wrap.
2. Turn out dough on lightly floured surface, pat down and fold twice. Pat down again. Fold again. Form into ball and let rise in bowl covered by plastic wrap until slightly more than doubled in bulk, about 2 hours.
3. Remove from bowl, pat down dough on lightly floured surface. Flour dough lightly, place on floured baking sheet and refrigerate 10-15 minutes. Roll out dough to ¹/₄-inch thickness and pat into buttered and floured 9-inch tart pan with removable bottom. Trim off excess, form into ball and roll out to ¹/₄-inch thickness for tart lid.
4. After filling tart, place dough-lid on top. Cut decorative pattern into top with sharp knife. Make egg wash by beating egg with 1 teaspoon water. Trim edges of tart lid, brush edges of top and bottom with some wash and pinch to seal. Brush top with remainder of wash.

5. Bake at 350° F for 1 hour, until golden brown. Cool 10-15 minutes before removing from tart pan. Serve warm or at room temperature.

Filling

6 ounces dried apricots, chopped
   coarsely
6 ounces dried prunes, chopped
   coarsely
1 onion, chopped finely
3 tablespoons butter
2 cloves garlic, minced
¹/₂ cup port
2 tablespoons brandy
1 tablespoon minced fresh sage
1 teaspoon dried savory
2 tart apples, peeled, cored and
   chopped finely
1 cup cranberries, rinsed and dried
¹/₂ pound smoked ham, ground coarsely
¹/₂ pound ground pork sausage
   Salt and pepper
10 ounces Gruyère cheese, shredded

1. Sauté apricots, prunes and onion in butter over medium heat until onion is soft, about 10 minutes. Add garlic and sauté 1 minute without browning. Add port and boil 2-3 minutes to reduce. Add brandy and boil 1-2 minutes, stirring, to thicken. Remove from heat and stir in sage and savory. Cool.
2. Mix apples, cranberries, ham and sausage. Mix in cooled dried fruit-onion mixture. Salt and pepper to taste. Mix in cheese.

Serves 6-10

BRAISED HAM WITH CRANBERRY SAUCE

Hams are nearly as popular during autumn and winter holidays as turkeys. Here's a simple method of bringing a juicy ham to table for a feast and giving it a Pacific Northwest flavor with an unusual cranberry sauce.

Use a fully cooked ham ("ready-to-eat") or a dry-cured ham. The latter will need soaking for at least 12 hours in cold water, scrubbing and simmering in water until a

meat thermometer pushed deep into the meat registers 150°F.

> 6 tablespoons butter
> 1 1/2 cups chopped onion
> 1 cup chopped carrots
> 3/4 cup chopped celery
> 1/4 cup chopped parsley
> 1 tablespoon chopped fresh thyme
> 8-to-10 pound ham, rind and most fat removed
> 2 1/2 cups dry white wine
> 8-12 cups meat stock (see Notes on Ingredients, page xi)
> 2 bay leaves
> Cranberry Sauce (recipe follows)

1. In covered roaster or heavy casserole just large enough to hold ham, melt butter and sauté onion, carrots, celery and parsley over medium heat until lightly browned. Stir in thyme.
2. Place ham on top of vegetables fat side up. Pour in wine and meat stock until liquid reaches halfway up the ham. Add bay leaves.
3. Bring liquid to boil on stove, cover and braise in 325°F oven for 1 hour, turning ham twice. Serve hot with Cranberry Sauce.

Serves 12-16

Cranberry Sauce

> 1 cup red currant jelly
> 1 cup orange juice
> 1/2 cup chopped onion
> 2 tablespoons balsamic vinegar
> 1 cup port
> 2 teaspoons Dijon mustard
> 12 ounces cranberries
> Zest of 1 orange
> Salt and pepper
> 1 teaspoon lemon juice

1. Bring jelly, orange juice, onion, vinegar, port and mustard to boil in saucepan. Stir to dissolve jelly. Turn heat to medium-low and simmer 10 minutes.
2. Coarsely chop half the cranberries and add to pan. Simmer until mixture thickens, about 15 minutes. Add remaining cranberries and orange zest and simmer until berries pop, about five minutes. Salt and pepper to taste. Stir in lemon juice. Cool to room temperature before serving.

SMOKED PORK WITH SPLIT PEA-POTATO PUREE

Central Europeans appreciate the nutritional and gustatory benefits of dried peas and lentils. This preparation, for instance, calls up the culinary glories of the Austro-Hungarian Empire. But the dried peas and Russet potatoes now come from that part of the Pacific Northwest called the Inland Empire: eastern Washington and western Idaho.

> 3 pounds smoked pork butt
> 1 cup finely diced bacon
> 1 large onion, chopped finely
> 5 cups chicken stock (see Notes on Ingredients, page xi)
> 1 1/4 pounds split green peas, rinsed and drained
> 3 large Russet potatoes, peeled and cut in medium chunks
> Salt and pepper
> 1 cup heavy cream
> 2 tablespoons butter, softened

1. Cover pork with water, bring to boil, turn heat to medium-low, partially cover and simmer 2 hours, or until quite tender. Stir occasionally to prevent sticking.
2. Meanwhile, sautè bacon over medium-low heat in heavy saucepan until fat has been rendered and bacon is lightly browned. Remove with slotted spoon and reserve. Sautè onion in bacon fat until soft and lightly colored, 10-12 minutes. Add stock, peas and bacon. Bring to boil, lower heat to low, cover and simmer 70 minutes, until peas are nearly tender. Add potatoes and simmer 15-20 minutes, until potatoes and peas are tender. Drain.
3. Puree potato-pea mixture in food mill or processor. Return to saucepan, salt and pepper to taste, beat in cream and butter, cover and simmer 4-5 minutes.
4. To serve, carve pork butt into thin slices and accompany with puree.

Serves 6-8

Grilled
Tenderloin of
Pork with
Grilled
Potatoes and
Apples

Pork Loin on
Bed of
Potatoes

GRILLED TENDERLOIN OF PORK WITH GRILLED POTATOES AND APPLES

Think of serving this dish on an Indian Summer evening, before storing the backyard barbecue for the winter. Pork tenderloin is not always available in supermarkets' meat cases, but a butcher should provide it.

> 2 cups Riesling
> 1/2 cup walnut oil
> 2 tablespoons light soy sauce
> 2 cloves garlic, slivered
> 2 teaspoons minced fresh ginger
> 10 juniper berries, pounded lightly
> 12 whole black peppercorns
> 1 tablespoon orange zest
> 2 pork tenderloins, about 3/4 pound each
> 2 Russet potatoes, sliced 1/4 inch thick
> 2 sweet potatoes, peeled and sliced 1/4 inch thick
> 2 apples, sliced 1/3 inch thick
> Salt to taste
> Rounds of French bread

1. Prepare marinade by combining wine, oil, soy sauce, garlic, ginger, juniper berries, peppercorns and orange zest. Place pork in glass dish just large enough to hold it. Pour on marinade, turn pork several times to coat well, cover dish with plastic wrap and refrigerate overnight, turning several times. Allow pork to come to room temperature in marinade before cooking.
2. Remove pork from marinade, reserving marinade. Grill pork over hot coals about 20 minutes, salting to taste and basting frequently with marinade.
3. Meanwhile, add potatoes, sweet potatoes and apples to marinade. Grill them alongside pork for about 10 minutes, basting frequently with marinade. Salt potatoes and sweet potatoes to taste.
4. Brush bread rounds with oil from top of marinade and toast on grill.

Serves 4-6

PORK LOIN ON BED OF POTATOES

Pork and fruit have an affinity. Here, a lean pork loin is first roasted with fruits and vegetables and then finished with Pacific Northwest Russet potatoes. The sauce that results is rich and flavorful.

> 3-pound boneless pork loin
> 2 heads garlic, cloves peeled and slivered
> Juice of 1 lemon
> 1 teaspoon salt
> 1/2 teaspoon pepper
> 1/2 teaspoon minced fresh sage
> 1/2 teaspoon minced fresh thyme
> Pinch allspice
> 1 large onion, chopped coarsely
> 1 apple, cored and chopped coarsely
> 2 cups cranberries
> 2 medium onions, sliced thinly
> 2 tablespoons butter
> 6 Russet potatoes, cut in 1/4-inch-thick slices
> Salt and pepper
> 2 cups strong meat stock (see Notes on Ingredients, page xi)
> 1/2 cup port

1. Make tiny cuts all over pork loin and insert slivers of garlic. Brush pork with lemon juice. Combine salt, pepper, sage, thyme and allspice and rub into meat. Place pork in a glass dish, cover with plastic wrap and marinate overnight, turning several times. Scrape off marinade before proceeding.
2. Allow pork to come to room temperature. Place fat side up in enameled casserole with tight-fitting cover just large enough to hold loin. Sear in 500°F oven for 20 minutes, turning meat three times to ensure even browning. Lower heat to 350°F, then scatter onion, apple and cranberries around and over loin. Roast 40 minutes, covered, basting 2 or 3 times during cooking.

3. While pork is roasting, sauté sliced onions in butter over medium-low heat until lightly colored. If potato slices were held in water, dry them well. Layer them in buttered shallow baking dish large enough to hold pork loin and fruits and vegetables. Salt and pepper potatoes to taste. Cover with onion slices. Heat meat stock to simmer and pour ¹/₂ cup on onions and potatoes.

4. Transfer roasted pork onto onion-potato bed. Generously moisten exposed potatoes with fat and juices from the roasting pan. Place baking dish in lower third of 350° F oven for 15 minutes, to glaze pork and cook potatoes.

5. Meanwhile, remove fruits and vegetables from roasting casserole to sieve. Holding sieve above casserole, press juices from solids with wooden spoon. Pour in remaining meat stock, place on stove over high heat and bring to boil, scraping up brown bits from bottom of casserole with wooden spoon. Add port and boil 5 minutes. Strain into small saucepan, skim fat and adjust seasoning. (Boil to reduce further if thicker sauce is desired.)

6. To serve, slice pork, moisten with sauce and accompany with potatoes.

Serves 6-8

FILLET OF BEEF STUFFED WITH WILD MUSHROOMS

The eastern half of the Pacific Northwest is cattle country. There, chaps are as common as slickers are along the coast. Not surprisingly, beef consumption remains high in the region, despite the rising popularity of seafood.

Here's a method of preparing a flavorful fillet for a large dinner party or a holiday feast. We think of this as a winter dish, when fresh wild mushrooms are hard to find. Many Pacific Northwestern mushroom hunters dry their harvests and can dip into reserves for this recipe. Dried morels and boletes are readily available in the market, however. (Dried boletes, imported and domestic, often are sold under their Italian name, *porcini*.)

> ¹/₂ cup olive oil
> 3 ¹/₄ cups dry red wine
> 3 cloves garlic, sliced
> 4 sprigs fresh rosemary
> 8-pound beef fillet, trimmed of fat
> 3 ounces dried morels or boletes (*porcini*)
> 2 cups hot meat stock (*see Notes on Ingredients, page xi*)
> 4 thin slices prosciutto
> Salt and pepper
> 1 pound pork fatback, sliced in ¹/₈-inch sheets

1. Mix olive oil, 3 cups wine, garlic and rosemary and thoroughly coat beef fillet. Marinate in glass baking dish for 2 hours at room temperature, turning meat several times.

2. Soak dried mushrooms in hot meat stock for 30 minutes. Drain and pat dry. Strain stock and reserve.

3. Remove fillet from marinade and pat dry. Slice lengthwise down the center through two-thirds of the thickness, stopping short of the thin tail. Spread fillet open and flatten slightly.

4. Stuff fillet by spreading on prosciutto and sprinkling on mushrooms, then garlic and rosemary from marinade. Salt and pepper to taste.

5. Fold tail of fillet toward middle to insure even cooking. Close fillet and cover with fatback. Tie with string at 1-inch intervals.

6. Roast fillet in shallow pan at 400° F. Figure 30 minutes for rare meat, or when meat thermometer registers 130° F. Allow roast to stand, covered with foil, for 15 minutes before slicing.

7. Degrease pan juices. Deglaze pan on stove with remaining ¹/₄ cup wine. Add reserved meat stock from mushroom soaking and boil to reduce slightly. Strain and serve hot with fillet.

Serves 10-14

POT ROAST WITH POTATO PANCAKES

Jean Scott, a Seattle friend, makes a superb pot roast. What elevate this dish to the sublime are the potato pancakes, made with Pacific Northwest Russets, that she serves with the roast. Crisp on the edges, brown all over, these savory circles are as straightforward and uncomplicated as the pot roast. Add steamed broccoli flavored with melted butter and you'll understand, or remember, why meat and potatoes was for so long the standard prescription for a North American dinner.

> 1 cup flour
> Salt and pepper
> Lemon pepper
> Garlic salt
> 3-pound pot roast
> 2 tablespoons vegetable oil
> 3 stalks celery, cut in ¹/₂-inch pieces
> 6 small onions, halved
> 4 carrots, cut in ¹/₄-inch pieces
> ¹/₄ pound medium-sized domestic
>   mushrooms
> 1 cup dry red wine
> Potato Pancakes (recipe follows)

1. Mix flour with seasonings to taste. Dredge meat in flour. Brown meat in oil over medium-high heat in heavy pan. Roast, covered, at 325°F for 90 minutes.
2. Scatter vegetables around roast and pour on wine. Cover and roast 90 minutes more, or until tender.

Serves 6-8

Potato Pancakes

> 2 large Russet potatoes, cut in small
>   pieces and placed in ice water
> 2 eggs
> 1 medium onion, cut in pieces
> 2 tablespoons flour
>   Salt and pepper
> 2 tablespoons minced parsley
>   Vegetable oil

1. Drain potatoes and pat dry with paper towels. Blend all ingredients except parsley and oil in food processor. (Or grate potatoes finely and beat ingredients together.) Stir in parsley.
2. Form thin 3-inch pancakes and fry over medium-high heat in skillet with lightly oiled bottom. Brown on one side and then the other. Serve warm.

BOISE BEEF STEW

Beef is big business in Idaho. Every spring, a group called the Idaho CowBelles sponsors a recipe contest to promote their favorite meat. As cooks have loosened traditional bonds, entrants have become bolder and bolder. A recipe from a few years ago that caught our fancy, however, was quite down-to-earth. Imagine weary cowboys sitting around a camp fire while the cook spoons up platefuls of a stew combining two ingredients that are plentiful on the range: beef and strong black coffee. They work wonderfully together, producing a rich, dark gravy that begs to be sopped up with oversized biscuits.

Florence Pharis called this Beef Brazilian when she devised the recipe. We adapted it slightly and gave it a new name in honor of Pharis's hometown. Serve it with biscuits or atop mashed potatoes, rice or noodles.

> 2 large onions, chopped finely
> ¹/₄ cup vegetable oil
> 1 clove garlic, minced
> 3 pounds round steak, cut in small
>   cubes
>   Salt and pepper
> 2 tablespoons butter
> ¹/₄ cup flour
> 1 cup dry red wine
> ¹/₂ tablespoon minced fresh oregano
> ¹/₂ tablespoon minced fresh rosemary
> 1 cup strong coffee

1. Sauté onion in vegetable oil over medium-low heat in heavy skillet until soft but not browned, about 10 minutes. Add garlic and sauté 1-2 minutes. Remove and reserve.
2. Raise heat to medium-high and brown beef cubes a few at a time, removing and setting aside as you go. Salt and pepper to taste.
3. Lower heat to medium and melt butter in skillet. Stir in flour until well blended, being careful not to burn. Add wine, herbs and coffee. Stir until slightly thickened. Return meat and onion mixture to skillet, bring to boil, turn heat to medium-low and simmer, covered, until meat is tender, about 70 minutes. Serve hot.

Serves 6

VEAL SWEETBREADS WITH CHANTERELLE SAUCE

Bruce Naftaly and Robin Sanders of Seattle were among the venturesome pioneers who made the breakthroughs leading to what is now known as Northwest Cooking. Seeking out what was fresh and representative of the region, encouraging cottage farmers to produce specialty vegetables and greens, urging fishermen and livestock and poultry producers to bring them their best, the two chefs introduced diners and cooks to the Pacific Northwest's rich culinary possibilities. Now happily running their own restaurant, Le Gourmand, in Seattle, Naftaly and Sanders display their careful style in this superb dish, with its rich sauce.

> 2 pounds sweetbreads
> 1 carrot, cut in small pieces
> 2 stalks celery, cut in small pieces
> 1 small onion, cut in small pieces
> 1 cup dry white wine
> 2 tablespoons clarified butter (see note)
> Salt
> 2 tablespoons cognac
> Chanterelle Sauce (recipe follows)

1. Rinse sweetbreads in cold water. Place in saucepan, cover with cold water and blanch by bringing to boil, skimming and boiling 1-2 minutes. Drain and rinse in cold water again.
2. Place vegetables and wine in a noncorrodible saucepan, cover and steam about 10 minutes, until vegetables are limp. Add sweetbreads and steam 10 minutes more. Remove sweetbreads and cool. (Reserve vegetables for making meat stock.)
3. Peel membranes from sweetbreads. Cut into 1/4-inch slices.
4. Sauté sweetbreads in the clarified butter over medium heat until golden brown on each side. Salt each side to taste while cooking. Remove to warm serving plates.
5. Add cognac to skillet to deglaze, scraping up brown bits. Add to Chanterelle Sauce. Spoon sauce over sweetbreads and serve hot.

Serves 4-6

Chanterelle Sauce

> 1 1/2 pounds chanterelles
> 1 cup dry white wine
> 2 tablespoons cognac
> 2 1/2 cups very strong meat stock (see Notes on Ingredients, page xi)
> 1 cup cognac
> 1 1/2 cups whipping cream
> Salt and white pepper

1. If mushrooms are large, halve lengthwise. Cut off stems and steam in wine and 2 tablespoons cognac in a noncorrodible pan until they release their liquid, about 15 minutes. Strain through sieve, pressing hard to obtain all liquid. Reserve liquid and discard stems.
2. Combine reserved mushroom liquid, meat stock and 1 cup cognac in a noncorrodible saucepan and boil to reduce to 1/2 cup. Add mushroom tops and cream and boil to thicken. Salt and pepper to taste.

Note: To clarify, melt 4 tablespoons butter over lowest heat in small saucepan. Carefully pour off melted butter, leaving milk solids behind.

Old-
Fashioned
Mincemeat

Hamburger,
Lentil and
Vegetable
Stew

Grilled Leg of
Lamb with
Apple-Mint
Chutney

OLD-FASHIONED MINCEMEAT

Central British Columbia, around Kam-loops, is cattle country. Roasts, ribs and chops are central to cooking there, and most families have favorite beef recipes, some handed down through many genera-tions. Here's one that draws on such tradi-tion: mincemeat, once an important part of North American cooking and now nearly forgotten.

The recipe comes from John Grace of Burns Lake, British Columbia. He freezes rather than cans it, and uses the savory mixture to make pies at holiday time.

Ask your butcher for the beef suet. He'll be surprised, since few people use suet any longer, but he'll readily supply it.

> 2 pounds cubed stew beef
> 1 pound beef suet, membranes removed
>   and chopped finely
> 1 pound candied fruit peel, chopped
>   finely
> 3 pounds apples, peeled, cored and
>   chopped coarsely
> 6 cups lightly packed dark brown sugar
> 4 cups apple cider
> 1 tablespoon nutmeg
> 1 tablespoon allspice
> 1 tablespoon ground cloves
> 1 tablespoon salt
> 2 tablespoons cinnamon
> 1 1/2 cups light molasses
> 6 cups dried black currants
> 3 cups dark raisins
> 3 cups golden raisins
> 2 cups brandy

1. Cover beef with water, bring to boil, lower heat and simmer until tender, about 90 minutes. Cool and chop coar-sely. Mix beef, suet, candied fruit peel and apples.
2. Bring sugar and cider to boil in a large pot. Lower heat and simmer 5 minutes, stirring to dissolve sugar. Remove from heat and stir in beef mixture and all other ingredients except brandy. Cool slightly before stirring in brandy. Refrigerate if using within a day or two. Otherwise, freeze until ready to use.

Makes about 6 quarts

HAMBURGER, LENTIL AND VEGETABLE STEW

Sherry Carter of Tensed, Idaho (wife of John, who is featured at the beginning of the Soups chapter) has developed many recipes featuring the lentils her husband harvests. The Carter children enjoy lentils because, Sherry says, they know "that's what Daddy grows."

Here's a Carter family favorite. "John did the spicing for this recipe," Sherry says. "So he should get some of the credit. It's quite thick, the way we like it. But some people might want to add some water to thin it a bit."

> 1 pound hamburger
> 1 medium onion, chopped coarsely
> 1 clove garlic, minced
> 4 cups canned tomatoes, drained and
>   pureed
> 1 1/2 cups tomato sauce
> 2 cups water
> 1 cup lentils
> 1/4 cup pearl barley
> 1 cup diced carrots
> 1 cup diced celery
> 1/4 cup chopped green pepper
> 1 cup fresh or frozen corn
> 1 cup fresh or frozen green beans
> 1 tablespoon garlic salt
> 1 teaspoon red pepper flakes
>   Salt and pepper

Brown hamburger, onion and garlic in large heavy-bottomed pot. Add tomatoes, tomato sauce and water and bring to boil. Add lentils and barley, lower heat and sim-mer 30 minutes. Add carrots, celery and green pepper and simmer 60 minutes more. Add corn, green beans, garlic salt, red pep-per flakes and salt and pepper to taste and simmer 30 minutes more.
Serves 6

GRILLED LEG OF LAMB WITH APPLE-MINT CHUTNEY

This is one of the best backyard-barbecue preparations we know. To make it easier, have your butcher trim the fat and fell from

the leg of lamb and then butterfly it, taking care that the meat is as even in thickness as possible. Save the marinade for further use by placing it in an airtight container in the refrigerator.

As accompaniments to the lamb, slice eggplant and zucchini paper thin, brush with olive oil and grill while the lamb rests after cooking.

> 3/4 cup olive oil
> Juice of 1 lemon
> 1/4 cup chopped fresh rosemary
> 1 tablespoon minced fresh oregano
> 3 bay leaves, crumbled
> 1 large onion, sliced thinly
> 4 cloves garlic, sliced
> Salt and pepper to taste
> 6- to 7-pound leg of lamb, fat and
>   fell removed and butterflied
> Apple-Mint Chutney (recipe follows)

1. Combine ingredients in a noncorrodible dish and marinate lamb for 30 hours, turning occasionally. (Refrigerate for first 24 hours, then continue marinating in cool part of the kitchen for 6 hours.) Scrape off marinade, strain and reserve for basting.
2. Grill lamb over medium-hot coals 15 minutes per side, basting occasionally with strained marinade. Slice into meat to test doneness and cook longer if desired.
3. Cover with foil and towel and allow to rest 10 minutes before carving. Slice against grain, dribble on a little marinade and serve warm with Apple-Mint Chutney.

Serves 6-8

Apple-Mint Chutney

> 1 bunch fresh mint (2 cups), chopped
>   finely
> 1 tart apple, peeled, cored and
>   chopped finely
> 1 Walla Walla Sweet onion,
>   chopped finely
> 1 jalapeno pepper, seeded and minced
> 1/2 cup olive oil
> 1/4 cup lime juice
> Salt and pepper to taste

Combine mint, apple, onion and pepper. Combine remaining ingredients and toss with mint mixture. Serve at room temperature.

BAKED CHICKEN WITH CARAMELIZED WALLA WALLA SWEETS

This is a wonderfully flavorful dish, easy to prepare and appetizing to view. The dark onions and black olives seem even richer against the brilliance of the lemons. Serve it with rice or mashed potatoes.

> 3-pound chicken, cut in serving pieces
> Flour for dredging, seasoned with
>   salt and pepper
> 2 tablespoons butter
> 2 tablespoons olive oil
> 4 large Walla Walla Sweet onions,
>   halved and cut in 1/4-inch slices
> 1 cup dry white wine
> 1/2 cup chicken stock (see Notes on
>   Ingredients, page xi)
> 12 cured black olives
> 1/2 teaspoon minced fresh thyme
> 1 bay leaf
> Salt and pepper
> 2 lemons, cut in wedges
> 1/4 cup minced parsley

1. Dredge chicken in seasoned flour. In heavy skillet, brown chicken in butter and olive oil over medium-high heat. Transfer with slotted spoon to baking dish in one layer.
2. In same skillet, over medium heat, sauté onions until soft and lightly browned, about 10 minutes. Spread onions on top of chicken.
3. Deglaze skillet with wine and chicken stock. Boil, scraping up brown bits from bottom, for 5 minutes. Pour over onions and chicken. Sprinkle on olives and thyme. Submerge bay leaf in liquid. Salt and pepper to taste. Scatter lemon wedges over all. Bake at 375° F for 40 minutes. Serve with sprinkle of parsley.

Serves 4

Grilled
Chicken with
Apricot-
Mustard
Glaze

Pressed
Chicken with
Salsa Verde

GRILLED CHICKEN WITH APRICOT-MUSTARD GLAZE

Long summer evenings draw Pacific Northwesterners outside to the barbecue. Faced, once again, with a couple of cut-up chickens, try this alternative to heavy barbecue sauces. Sweet-hot in flavor, the glaze becomes an appetizing gold on the grill.

> 1/3 cup olive oil
> 1 1/2 cups dry white wine
> 3 cloves garlic, crushed
>   Salt and pepper
> 1 chicken, cut in quarters
>   Apricot-Mustard Glaze
>   (recipe follows)

1. Mix olive oil, wine, garlic and salt and pepper to taste. Place chicken in glass dish and pour on marinade. Turn pieces to coat well and marinate in refrigerator for 4 hours. Bring to room temperature before cooking. Drain chicken and pat dry.
2. Grill chicken about 35 minutes over medium-hot coals, turning often. A few minutes before chicken is cooked, brush several times with Apricot-Mustard Glaze. Serve with additional glaze at the table as a sauce.

Serves 4

Apricot-Mustard Glaze

> 1/2 pound dried apricots
> 3 cups water
> 1/2 cup minced shallots
> 4 tablespoons butter
> 2/3 cup white wine vinegar
> 2/3 cup rice wine vinegar
> 1 cup honey
> 2 teaspoons salt
> 1 teaspoon white pepper
> 1/4 cup hot mustard

1. Bring apricots and water to a boil, lower heat and simmer 15 minutes, until liquid is reduced by half.
2. Meanwhile, sauté shallots in butter over medium-low heat until soft, about 10 minutes.
3. Puree apricots in their liquid in blender or food processor. Add shallots and remaining ingredients and mix until well blended but not liquid.

PRESSED CHICKEN WITH SALSA VERDE

A tribute to the Pacific Northwest mint business, this is a dramatic and flavorful method of serving chicken. The birds come out of the oven moist, appetizingly golden and with their parts nicely spread out. For full effect, cut them into serving portions at table.

Begin by wrapping two bricks in heavy foil. Then proceed as below.

> 2 3-pound chickens
> 1/2 cup chopped mint
> 2 cloves garlic, minced
>   Juice of 1 lemon
>   Salt and pepper
> 1/2 cup olive oil
>   Salsa Verde (recipe follows)

1. Remove backbones from chickens by cutting down one side of spine and then the other, peeling back skin to expose bones. Skin side down, split an inch or so of the upper breastbone cartilage and then press with hands to flatten whole chicken.
2. Combine mint, garlic, lemon juice and salt and pepper to taste. Whisk in olive oil. Bathe chickens in marinade and marinate in refrigerator overnight. Marinate 1 hour at room temperature before cooking.
3. Heat the two bricks in 400° F oven for 30 minutes. Remove and brush one wide side of each with olive oil. Line heavy baking sheet with heavy foil and brush with olive oil. Place chickens skin side up on the prepared baking sheet. Place a brick, oiled side down, on each chicken.

4. Roast in upper third of oven at 375°F
   for 20 minutes. Remove bricks, baste
   chickens with pan juices and roast 10-
   15 minutes more, until chickens are
   golden-colored. Serve hot or at room
   temperature with Salsa Verde. (In the
   latter case, baste several times as
   chickens cool.)

Serves 6-8

Salsa Verde

1 slice French or Italian bread
2 tablespoons red wine vinegar
1 red pepper, roasted and cut in small
     dice (see Notes on
     Ingredients, page xi)
1 medium onion, cut in small dice
2 tablespoons capers, rinsed, drained
     and chopped coarsely
3 cloves garlic, minced
1/2 cup minced Italian parsley
2 teaspoons minced fresh oregano
3 tablespoons balsamic vinegar
3/4 cup olive oil, preferably extra-virgin
1 hard-boiled egg, chopped finely
     Salt and pepper

1. Soak bread in vinegar. Squeeze out excess. Puree.
2. Mix bread and all other ingredients except olive oil, egg and salt and pepper.
   Whisk in olive oil in a thin stream. Mix
   in egg and salt and pepper to taste.

CHICKEN WITH
ASPARAGUS AND MORELS

Spring brings an ample supply of Pacific
Northwest asparagus and superb morel
mushrooms. What better way to celebrate
the season than by combining the two in
this one-dish meal? Sweet turnips and deli-
cately anise-flavored fennel complete the
medley and form a light background to show
off the dark morel nuggets and brilliant
asparagus pieces.

1 small onion, halved and sliced thinly
1 stalk celery, sliced thinly
1 small carrot, peeled and sliced thinly
3 tablespoons butter
2 tablespoons olive oil
4 pounds chicken pieces
4 tablespoons flour
     Salt and pepper
4 cups chicken stock, boiling
2 sprigs fresh thyme, 2 sprigs fresh
     tarragon, 1 bay leaf, tied
     with string
1 pound asparagus, cut diagonally in
     1-inch pieces
4 small fennel bulbs, quartered
1/2 pound morels, halved if large
4 small turnips, peeled and cut in
     1-inch batons
1/2 cup chopped fresh basil
2 tablespoons butter

1. Sauté onion, celery and carrot in the
   butter and olive oil over medium heat
   in a large skillet until soft, about 7
   minutes. Remove with slotted spoon
   and reserve.
2. Raise heat to medium-high and brown
   chicken pieces in the same skillet. Turn
   heat to medium-low, cover skillet and
   cook 10 minutes, turning chicken once.
3. With heat still on, sprinkle chicken
   with flour and salt and pepper to taste,
   turning chicken to coat evenly. Pour in
   boiling chicken stock and shake pan to
   blend flour and stock. Add herb bundle
   and more stock, if necessary, to nearly
   submerge chicken. Cover and simmer
   30 minutes, until chicken is tender.
4. Ten minutes before chicken is cooked,
   add sautéed vegetables, asparagus, fennel, morels, turnips and basil. Just
   before serving, stir in the final 2
   tablespoons butter and baste chicken
   with sauce. Serve hot.

Serves 4-6

STUFFED CHICKEN BREASTS WITH CIDER SAUCE

This stuffing is so good that you might want to double the recipe, bake the extra stuffing in a greased loaf pan covered with foil, slice it and serve as an accompaniment to the chicken breasts. (One hour at 350° F.)

The chicken breasts serve equally well as a main course, with the cider sauce, or as part of a cold buffet. In the latter case, refrigerate them first while still rolled in their foil packets. When they're well chilled, remove foil and slice diagonally.

If your butcher bones the chicken breasts for you, have him remove the tenderloins and give them to you. Use two or three of them in the stuffing and freeze the remainder.

> 3 whole chicken breasts, boned, skinned
>   and left in one piece
> 3 large, thin slices smoked ham
> 2 cloves garlic, minced
> 3 shallots, minced
> 1/2 cup minced onion
> 1 stalk celery, chopped finely
> 1 cup peeled, cored and finely
>   chopped apple
> 4 tablespoons butter
> 1/4 pound chicken breast (use breast
>   tenderloins), chopped
> 1/2 pound Italian sausage, casings
>   removed
> 1/4 cup cassis liqueur
> 2 tablespoons apple brandy
> 1 teaspoon minced fresh marjoram
> 1/2 teaspoon minced fresh sage
> 1/8 teaspoon allspice
>   Salt and pepper
> 2 eggs
> 1/2 cup heavy cream
> 1/2 cup apple cider
> 2 cups coarse fresh bread crumbs
> 1/2 cup finely chopped walnuts
>   Cider Sauce (recipe follows)

1. Remove tenderloins from breasts. Reserve 2-3 for stuffing. Between sheets of waxed paper, pound upper parts of breasts lightly to flatten and make more even in thickness with bottom parts. Lay ham slices on inside part of breasts.

2. Sauté garlic, shallots, onion, celery and apple in butter over medium-low heat until soft but not brown, about 10 minutes. Chill in refrigerator.

3. Grind chicken tenderloins and sausage together. Or mince in food processor whose bowl, top and blade have been chilled in freezer for 15 minutes. If using food processor, keep motor running and add cassis and apple brandy. Stop motor and scrape down sides. Add marjoram, sage, allspice and salt and pepper to taste. Turn on motor and pulse to combine well. Add eggs and pulse to blend. With machine running, pour in cream and cider. Transfer to mixing bowl.

4. If not using food processor, after grinding chicken and sausage, beat in ingredients by hand, blending thoroughly at each step.

5. In mixing bowl, fold in bread crumbs and mix well. Mix in sautéed vegetables. Fold in walnuts. Taste for seasoning by sautéing a tablespoon of mixture in a little butter. (Stuffing may be prepared a day in advance and refrigerated until ready to use.)

6. Spread stuffing evenly on ham-lined chicken breasts. Beginning with widest part, roll up breasts firmly. Place each in middle of an oiled square of foil with shiny side up. Tuck one edge of foil tightly under chicken cylinder and then roll up chicken in foil, twisting ends to seal.

7. Place foil rolls on baking sheet and bake at 400° F for 15 minutes. Turn off oven, open door and allow chicken packets to sit in oven 15 minutes. Remove foil, slice diagonally and serve warm with Cider Sauce.

Serves 6-8

Cider Sauce

3 cups apple cider
¹/₂ cup white wine vinegar
¹/₂ cup cassis liqueur
¹/₂ cup apple brandy
¹/₂ cup strong chicken stock
1 ¹/₂ cups heavy cream
Salt and pepper

1. Boil cider in saucepan to reduce to 1 cup. In another saucepan, boil vinegar and cassis to reduce to ¹/₄ cup. Combine reduced cider, reduced vinegar mixture, apple brandy and chicken stock and boil to reduce to ³/₄ cup.
2. Add cream and simmer briskly to reduce until mixture thickens and coats a wooden spoon, about 20 minutes. Salt and pepper to taste. (Sauce can be prepared in advance and brought to simmer before serving.)

CHICKEN BREASTS WITH RASPBERRY-TERIYAKI SAUCE

Leif Eric Benson, executive chef of Timberline Lodge on Oregon's Mt. Hood, finds this dish to be among the most popular on his menu. The familiar teriyaki sauce draws character and tartness from the raspberries, and the color is dramatic. Benson likes to spoon the sauce on serving plates to form a background for the rolled chicken breasts and then garnish with a few whole berries.

6 skinned and boned chicken breasts
6 thin slices Danish ham
6 hearts of palm
Salt and pepper

Sauce

2 tablespoons finely diced onion
1 clove garlic, minced
2 tablespoons olive oil
2 tablespoons ketchup
1 cup pineapple juice
¹/₄ cup light soy sauce
2 tablespoons dark brown sugar
2 tablespoons red wine vinegar
1 tablespoon freshly grated ginger
1 teaspoon dry mustard
3 ¹/₂ teaspoons arrowroot
1 tablespoon cold water
1 cup red raspberries

1. Pound chicken breasts gently between sheets of waxed paper until ¹/₄ inch thick. Wrap ham slices around hearts of palm, then roll up in chicken breasts. Salt and pepper to taste. Bake on lightly oiled baking sheet at 375° F for about 20 minutes, until just done.
2. To prepare sauce, sauté onion and garlic in olive oil over medium heat until lightly colored. Stir in remaining ingredients except arrowroot, water and raspberries. Mix arrowroot with water. Mix in tablespoon or so of the warm sauce, then add arrowroot mixture to sauce. Stir and cook until slightly thickened.
3. Remove from heat and fold in raspberries. Serve warm with chicken breasts.

Serves 6

**Duck with
Sweet
Cherries**

**Breast of
Duck with
Plum Sauce**

DUCK WITH SWEET CHERRIES

Duck and fruit are joined in many cuisines. This combination, for instance, goes back a long way in French cooking. Pacific Northwestern cooks draw their inspiration from many sources, but they don't need to borrow sweet cherries. The region's orchards produce the finest anywhere.

If you want to make this dish when cherries aren't in season, substitute dried cherries, now widely available in specialty food shops. Because they are so concentrated in flavor, use only ³/₄ cup.

> 5-pound duck
> Salt and pepper
> 1 small onion, halved
> ¹/₂ tart apple
> 1 pound fresh sweet cherries, pitted
> ¹/₄ cup kirsch
> 1 tablespoon lemon juice
> ¹/₂ cup minced onion
> ¹/₄ cup minced carrot
> 2 tablespoons butter
> 1 cup dry red wine
> 2 cups chicken stock (see Notes on
>   Ingredients, page xi)
> 1 tablespoon minced fresh marjoram
> Salt and pepper
> 2 tablespoons butter, softened

1. Season duck's cavity with salt and pepper. Place onion and apple inside cavity. Roast breast-side up at 425°F for 15 minutes, until lightly browned. Remove from oven and cool. Cut in quarters, trimming excess fat and scraping exposed bones.
2. Bring cherries, kirsch and lemon juice to boil in small saucepan. Turn off heat and let rest 30 minutes.
3. Sauté onion and carrot in butter over medium-low heat in large skillet until soft but not browned, about 5 minutes. Add duck and wine, raise heat and boil for 1-2 minutes. Add chicken stock, marjoram and salt and pepper to taste, turn heat to medium-low and simmer for 40 minutes, until duck is tender. Remove duck to warm platter.
4. Strain liquids from skillet, degrease, add cherry mixture and boil until slightly thickened, about 10 minutes. Lower heat to medium and stir in the final 2 tablespoons butter. Pour sauce over duck and serve.

Serves 4

BREAST OF DUCK WITH PLUM SAUCE

Large, black, amber-fleshed Friar plums ripen in midsummer in the Pacific Northwest. They're wonderful to eat fresh, but they also cook well, as in this sauce.

A perfect accompaniment for the duck breasts and their rich, slightly sweet sauce is a mixture of strong-flavored greens that have been blanched and then sautéed in olive oil with a mince of garlic and pancetta or ham.

Plum Sauce

> 1 cup chicken stock (see Notes on
>   Ingredients, page xi)
> ¹/₂ cup plus 2 tablespoons blueberry
>   vinegar
> ¹/₄ cup brandy
> 4 Friar plums, pitted and cut into
>   6 wedges
> 1 cup heavy cream
> Salt and pepper

1. Boil chicken stock to reduce to ¹/₂ cup.
2. Boil ¹/₂ cup vinegar and brandy to reduce to ¹/₂ cup. Add stock and boil 2 minutes. Add plum wedges, lower heat to medium and poach 2 minutes. Remove with slotted spoon and reserve. Raise heat and boil sauce to reduce to ¹/₂ cup.
3. Add cream and boil to thicken, until sauce coats the back of a wooden spoon. Salt and pepper to taste and add additional vinegar if more tartness is desired. Return plums to sauce and heat through. Serve hot.

Duck Breasts

> 3 whole duck breasts, skinned, boned
>   and halved
> 3 tablespoons clarified butter (see note)
>   Salt and pepper

Sauté duck in clarified butter over medium-high heat, adding salt and pepper to taste, until medium-rare, about 8 minutes. Slice thinly and serve hot in a puddle of sauce, with more sauce spooned on top. Serves 6

Note: *To clarify, melt 4 tablespoons butter over lowest heat in small saucepan. Carefully pour off melted butter, leaving milk solids behind.*

BREAST OF DUCK ON POTATO PANCAKES WITH CRANBERRY VINAIGRETTE

The brilliant Cranberry Vinaigrette, the caramel-colored duck breasts and the golden-brown potato pancakes make this a dish of appetizing colors. Complete the palette by serving an accompaniment of sautéed spinach flavored with garlic.

> 3 whole duck breasts, boned, with
>   skin left on
>   Salt and pepper
> 3 medium Russet potatoes, peeled
> 2 tablespoons butter
> 1 tablespoon vegetable oil
>   Cranberry Vinaigrette (recipe follows)

1. Salt and pepper duck breasts to taste. Place on rack in roasting pan skin side up and roast 10 minutes at 450° F. Set aside while preparing potato pancakes.
2. Grate potatoes coarsely into ice water. Squeeze out water and pat dry between paper towels.
3. Divide potatoes into 6 portions. Between sheets of waxed paper, flatten portions into ¼-inch-thick pancakes about 6 inches in diameter.
4. Sauté pancakes in butter over medium-low heat about 8 minutes. When pancake holds its shape, flip and cook about 3 minutes. Salt and pepper both sides to taste. Keep warm until ready to serve.
5. Finish cooking duck breasts by frying in vegetable oil over high heat skin side down about 3 minutes, being careful not to burn. Lower heat to medium, cover and cook until medium-rare, about 5 minutes. Let rest 10 minutes, covered loosely with foil, before slicing diagonally.
6. To serve, fan slices of duck breast over potato pancake and spoon on Cranberry Vinaigrette.

Serves 6

Cranberry Vinaigrette

> 6 ounces cranberries
> ½ cup sugar
>   Juice of 1 orange
> ¾ cup berry vinegar
> 2 tablespoons lemon juice
> ¼ cup honey
> ¼ cup Dijon mustard
> ¼ cup walnut oil
> ½ cup vegetable oil
>   Salt and pepper

1. Spread berries in buttered noncorrodible baking dish just large enough to hold berries in one layer. Sprinkle with sugar. Cover tightly with foil and bake at 350° F for 20 minutes. Remove foil and cool.
2. Puree cranberries in food mill or processor. In blender or food processor, mix in orange juice, vinegar, lemon juice, honey and mustard. With machine running, add oils in a thin, steady stream. Salt and pepper to taste. Warm in saucepan before serving.

WILLAMETTE VALLEY

Where Dreams Are Rooted in the Soil

For the farmers who endured the rigors of the Oregon Trail, the Willamette Valley of Oregon must have seemed a dream. Beginning in the Calapooya Mountains south of what today is the city of Eugene, the valley gradually spread out as its river flowed 170 miles north to join the Columbia. Flanked by the Coast Ranges to the west and the Cascades to the east, the valley had its own special climate and offered plenty of room to grow. Because the Coast Ranges partially blocked the flow of moist marine air, the Willamette Valley was warmer, drier and sunnier than western Washington and British Columbia. In those areas, pioneers found towering forests of fir. In the Willamette, they found open grassland, prairie, savanna and forests of oak as well as fir. Here was a place where a farmer could put down roots.

The valley still seems a dream. Other industries have found homes in the Willamette since the pioneer days, but agriculture continues to be its main business. Tree fruits, dairy and beef cattle, hay, vegetables, grass seed, strawberries, hazelnuts and wine grapes all grow there with distinction. The valley's special pride, however, is the crop known awkwardly as caneberries.

Caneberries grow from plants whose wood resembles canes. Consumers know them as raspberries and blackberries. To Pacific Northwesterners, especially those living

SIDE DISHES

91

west of the Cascade Mountains, caneberries are as familiar as salmon and fir trees. Come summer, the berries ripen in backyards and along roadways, and commercial growers ship them to markets in a variety of dazzling colors and sizes. To outsiders, however, caneberries–particularly the blackberries–can be rare culinary jewels.

Caneberries grow in many parts of North America. Only in the Pacific Northwest, however, do they grow in such profusion and have such commercial value. British Columbia, Washington and Oregon account for most of the commercial supply of red raspberries. Oregon alone grows most of the black raspberries. And between them, Oregon and Washington grow most of the commercial blackberries.

The blackberry business is undergoing rapid change. Blackberries easily hybridize; there are some 450 varieties with names, and thousands without names, just numbers. Some varieties pop up on their own, chance mutations.

One such mutation, called Boysenberry after the scientist who identified it, now ranks as the prince of blackberries. The gustatory attributes of this huge berry were a Pacific Northwest secret until the flavored-yogurt business spread its fame across the country. Now, though it's expensive to grow and harvest, the Boysenberry is much in demand.

In the early days of the Willamette's caneberry business, the prince among berries was the Loganberry, a raspberry-blackberry cross. Large and tart but soft and short-lived off the cane, Loganberries were planted alongside the Willamette's rail lines so they could be picked, packed in bar-

rels with sulfur as a preservative and shipped by rail to market. The Loganberry is rapidly disappearing, however, its place being taken by firmer berries that last longer.

Fresh-market demand for Pacific Northwest caneberries is dramatically on the rise. Consumers in the East and Midwest clamor for berries during the summer, and Willamette growers are heeding the call. Thornless Evergreen blackberries and the hybrid known as Marionberry–a large berry with a nice tart-sweet balance–make up the bulk of their blackberry crop. But new berries with complex flavors, good size and comely shape, such as the Kotata and Waldo, are being planted to meet the fresh-market demand.

"Caneberries are like wines," says Esther Nelson, an Easterner who arrived in the Willamette Valley to learn about vegetables and instead got caught up in the berry business. "Each has its own distinctive flavor, and it doesn't make sense to compare them. Just enjoy them all."

Among the variety of provender from Oregon's Willamette Valley (see overleaf) are the hazelnuts in this chutney, which also includes mint and black currants among its local ingredients (recipe on page 96). It is meant as an accompaniment for meat, fish, cold cuts and cheese.

SIDE DISHES

ASPARAGUS AND POTATO PUREE

Flavorful and colorful, this marriage of two of the Pacific Northwest's splendid vegetables accompanies roasted or grilled meats, poultry and fish as appropriately as mashed potatoes. In order to get the proper texture, the asparagus must be sweated in butter rather than boiled or steamed. It's also a good idea to peel the stalks, even after breaking off the tough ends.

> 1 pound Russet potatoes, peeled and cut in chunks
> 1 onion, cut in chunks
> 1 pound asparagus, cut in 1-inch pieces
> 8 tablespoons butter, softened
> 1 tablespoon minced mint
> Salt and pepper
> 2 teaspoons lemon juice
> $^1/_2$ cup heavy cream

1. Boil potatoes and onion together until tender. Drain.
2. Meanwhile, stir-fry asparagus in 4 tablespoons of the butter over medium heat for about 5 minutes. (Asparagus should retain some crunchiness.)
3. Puree potatoes, onion and asparagus in food mill or processor. Beat in mint, salt and pepper to taste and lemon juice. Beat in cream until just blended. Reheat in saucepan placed in larger pan containing 2-3 inches of simmering water. Beat in remaining butter.

Serves 6-8

POTATO PUDDING

Potato casserole recipes are nearly as numerous in Washington and Idaho potato-growing areas as the spuds themselves. Here's an example of the species, an easy preparation that provides an alternative to plain baked, mashed or fried potatoes.

> 6 medium Russet potatoes, peeled and grated into ice water
> 1 medium onion, chopped finely
> 1 cup milk
> 6 tablespoons butter
> Salt and white pepper
> 3 eggs, beaten
> $^1/_2$ cup sliced almonds, lightly toasted in dry skillet

1. Squeeze moisture from potatoes. Mix with onion.
2. Warm milk and butter over medium heat until butter melts. Salt and pepper to taste. Gradually stir eggs into mixture.
3. Spread potato mixture in buttered baking dish. Pour in egg-milk mixture. Sprinkle with toasted almonds. Bake at 350°F about 1 hour, until well browned.

Serves 6-8

BAKED POTATOES WITH ROASTED GARLIC AND GOAT CHEESE

Pacific Northwest Russets are the finest baking potatoes available because the long, sunny days and cool nights of the potato-growing areas produce large, solid tubers.

The blandness of potatoes encourages experimentation with toppings. Here's one that combines mellow roasted garlic with goat cheese and the traditional baked-potato toppings of butter, sour cream and chives.

> 2 heads garlic
> 2 tablespoons olive oil
> 2 sprigs fresh thyme
> Salt and pepper
> 6 ounces cream cheese
> 6 ounces goat cheese
> 4 tablespoons butter, softened
> $^1/_4$ cup sour cream
> 2 teaspoons Dijon mustard
> 2 tablespoons minced fresh chives
> Salt and pepper

1. Rub garlic heads with olive oil. Place thyme in small oven-proof container just large enough to hold garlic. Place garlic on top of thyme and sprinkle with remaining oil. Salt and pepper lightly.
2. Bake at 300°F for 30 minutes, until garlic cloves become soft. Squeeze out garlic from each clove. Remove thyme leaves from stems and add to garlic. Puree in food mill or processor. Beat in cheeses, butter, sour cream and mustard until smooth. Fold in chives. Salt and pepper to taste. Chill at least 2 hours. Serve at room temperature atop baked potatoes.

Makes topping for 4-6 potatoes

Baked Potatoes

> 4 large Russet potatoes, scrubbed
> Vegetable oil (optional)

Rub potatoes with oil if a soft skin is desired. Pierce several times with a fork to create steam vents. Bake at 400°F for 50 to 60 minutes, until potatoes feel soft. Slit lengthwise and push ends toward the middle to expose flesh. (Wrapping potatoes in foil before cooking is not desirable, resulting in something like a steamed potato rather than the dry, fluffy texture that characterizes a baked potato.)

HERBED BROILED POTATOES

With roasted or grilled meats, potatoes seem essential. Here's a quick method of transforming Pacific Northwest Russets into golden moons speckled with fresh green herbs.

> 4 Russet potatoes, peeled and sliced 1/4 inch thick
> Olive oil
> Salt and pepper
> 1/4 cup minced fresh basil
> 1 tablespoon minced fresh oregano
> 1 teaspoon minced fresh rosemary
> Red wine vinegar (optional)

1. Toss potato slices with olive oil to coat. Oil baking sheet. Lay potato slices, overlapping slightly, on baking sheet. Salt and pepper to taste.
2. Broil 6 inches from heat for about 10 minutes, until golden brown. Flip potatoes, brush with olive oil, salt and pepper to taste and broil until golden brown.
3. Sprinkle cooked potatoes with mixed herbs. Splash with vinegar if desired.

Serves 4-6

POTATO-CHEDDAR CASSEROLE

Baking potatoes and cheese together is common enough. Generally, however, milk is added. Here chicken stock is substituted to create a dish of a different flavor. Use mild, sharp or extra-sharp cheddar, according to taste.

> 1 large onion, sliced thinly
> 2 tablespoons butter
> 2 pounds Russet potatoes, peeled and sliced thinly
> 1/2 cup grated cheddar
> Nutmeg
> Salt and pepper
> 1 cup chicken stock (see Notes on Ingredients, page xi)

1. Sauté onion in butter over medium-low heat until quite soft, about 8 minutes.
2. Layer onion, potatoes and cheese in buttered baking dish, seasoning with nutmeg, salt and pepper to taste as you go. Pour on chicken stock. Bake, covered, at 350°F for about 1 hour, or until potatoes are tender. Remove cover, place under broiler 4 inches from heat in closed oven and broil until lightly browned.

Serves 4-6

Tomato-
Hazelnut
Chutney

Cranberry
Chutney

Cherry
Chutney

TOMATO-HAZELNUT CHUTNEY

Among the many recipes in this book developed by Tina Bell at her Seattle delicatessen, The Wedge, none is more popular than this condiment. Customers use it as an accompaniment for meats, fish, cold cuts and cheese. It will keep in the refrigerator tightly covered for several weeks. Or preserve in hot-water bath according to standard procedure.

> 1 cup mint leaves
> 5 large tomatoes, peeled, seeded and chopped coarsely (or 30 ounces canned Italian tomatoes, drained of most juice)
> 1 1/2 cups sugar
> 1 cup red wine vinegar
> 1/2 cup raspberry vinegar
> 6 cloves garlic, minced
> 2 teaspoons salt
> Pinch red pepper flakes
> 1 cup hazelnuts
> 1/2 cup dried black currants

1. Blanch mint leaves in boiling water for 1 minute, drain, rinse in cold water, squeeze dry and chop finely.
2. Combine all ingredients except hazelnuts and currants in noncorrodible pot. Bring to boil, turn heat to low and simmer 30-40 minutes, until mixture becomes quite thick. Add hazelnuts and currants after 20 minutes. Serve chilled. (Flavor improves after 2-3 days in refrigerator.)

Makes about 6 cups

CRANBERRY CHUTNEY

Cranberry sauce seems to be a holiday treat, while cranberry chutney has a year-round appeal. This is a beautiful condiment that goes well with pork, ham, poultry and even salmon. It can be kept for two weeks in the refrigerator. Or it can be frozen or preserved in hot-water bath according to standard procedures.

The 5-Spice powder can be found in Asian markets.

> 36 ounces cranberries, rinsed and dried
> 3 cups sugar
> 1 cup raspberry vinegar
> 2 cups cider vinegar
> 1 lemon, peeled and chopped coarsely
> 1 cup brown sugar
> 1 cup sugar
> 1 teaspoon salt
> 1/2 teaspoon cayenne pepper
> 2 teaspoons 5-Spice powder
> 1 teaspoon cinnamon
> 1 cup dried apricots, chopped in 1/4-inch pieces
> 1 cup chopped walnuts

1. Spread two-thirds of the cranberries on buttered baking sheets in one layer. Sprinkle evenly with the 2 cups sugar. Cover tightly with foil and bake at 350°F for 45 minutes. Open one corner of the foil to let steam escape.
2. Bring vinegars, lemon, brown sugar, 1 cup sugar, salt, cayenne, 5-Spice and cinnamon to boil. Lower heat to medium and simmer for 20 minutes, until slightly thickened.
3. Add remaining cranberries, apricots and walnuts. Simmer for 10 minutes. Mix in baked cranberries and simmer for 5 minutes. Chill. (Flavor improves after 2-3 days in refrigerator.)

Makes about 2 quarts

CHERRY CHUTNEY

The Pacific Northwest's mild, dry climate on the eastern slopes of the mountain ranges sheltering its interior is ideal for growing sweet cherries. Maroon Bings and Lamberts are the most common, but the dramatically colored Rainier–creamy white, with a golden-pink blush–draws a lot of attention during its short, sweet season.

Fruit chutneys are excellent accompaniments to pork, ham, poultry, game and cold cured meats. They also can be mixed with mayonnaise (preferably homemade) for salad and sandwich dressings. They can be kept refrigerated for two or more weeks or preserved in hot-water bath according to standard procedures.

2 cups cider vinegar
2 cups firmly packed dark brown sugar
1 tablespoon minced garlic
1 tablespoon minced onion
1 tablespoon minced fresh ginger
1 tablespoon dry mustard
1 tablespoon seeded, minced jalapeno
    pepper
10 whole cloves
1 teaspoon cinnamon
1/2 teaspoon salt
1 teaspoon pepper
2 quarts fresh sweet cherries, pitted
1 cup almonds, chopped coarsely

Boil vinegar and brown sugar in a non-corrodible pot for 15 minutes. Add all other ingredients except cherries and almonds, turn heat to low and simmer 10 minutes. Add cherries and simmer 30 minutes, until mixture has consistency of jam but cherries still retain some of their shape. Stir often to prevent burning, adding water if necessary. Stir in almonds 10 minutes before cooking is finished. Serve chilled. (Flavor improves after 2-3 days in refrigerator.)
Makes about 2 quarts

CRANBERRY-APPLE RELISH

Baking cranberries for relish seems to bring out their flavor and preserve their shape better than cooking them on top of the stove. Adding apples is appropriate in the Pacific Northwest. Use Golden Delicious, which retain their shape well under heat. Reduce the amount of sugar if a tart relish is desired.

An accompaniment to turkey or other poultry, this is also an excellent condiment for pork, ham or game. Serve it warm, at room temperature or chilled.

12 ounces cranberries, rinsed
1 1/2 cup sugar
2 apples, peeled, cored and cut into
    1/2-inch cubes
2 tablespoons butter
1/2 cup water
1/2 cup blueberry vinegar
    Pinch salt
1 cup walnuts, oven toasted and
    chopped coarsely

1. Place cranberries in one layer in large buttered baking pan or cookie sheet. Sprinkle evenly with sugar to taste. Cover tightly with foil and bake at 350° F for 45 minutes. Loosen corner of foil to release steam, but keep berries warm.
2. Sauté apples in butter over medium heat for about 5 minutes. They should still be slightly crisp. Mix apples with cranberries.
3. In same skillet, boil water, vinegar, salt and 1/2 tablespoon sugar until liquid is reduced to 2 tablespoons. Pour over cranberries and apples. Add walnuts and mix gently.
Makes 4 cups

PLUM CHUTNEY

A sweet-hot condiment that goes well with grilled meats and poultry, this chutney takes advantage of the Pacific Northwest's ample supply of inexpensive Italian Prune plums. It can be refrigerated for two weeks or preserved in hot-water bath according to standard procedures.

4 cups cider vinegar
2 cups sugar
1 tablespoon salt
1 teaspoon ground cloves
1 teaspoon cinnamon
1 teaspoon allspice
1 tablespoon minced fresh ginger
3 pounds Italian Prune plums, pitted
    and quartered
1 pound tart apples, peeled, cored and
    cut in 1/2-inch dice
2 medium onions, chopped coarsely
2 jalapeno peppers, seeded and minced
1/2 pound raisins
1 cup mint leaves, chopped
    Pepper

Boil vinegar, sugar, salt and spices in a noncorrodible pot for 10 minutes. Add fruits, onion, peppers and raisins, turn heat to medium-low and simmer until thick, about 30 minutes. Add mint and pepper to taste after 20 minutes of cooking.
Makes about 2 quarts.

APRICOT APPLESAUCE

Different apples produce different sauces. Golden Delicious, for instance, produce a mild-flavored sauce that is sweet enough (if the apples are ripe) without sugar. Granny Smiths produce a sour, aromatic sauce. Both varieties are widely available year-round. The ultimate sauce apple, Gravenstein, produces a tart, fresh-flavored sauce with a fluffy texture. Unfortunately, Gravenstein production is limited and the apple doesn't store well, so it's seen in markets only in late summer and early fall.

Any good sauce apple will do for this golden-hued, sweet-hot accompaniment to pork or poultry. Fresh horseradish is worth the effort to obtain, but the prepared product may be substituted.

> 3 pounds apples, peeled, cored and
>   quartered
> 1/2 pound dried apricots
> 1 cup water
> Sugar
> Salt
> Freshly grated horseradish
>   (or prepared)

1. Bring apples, apricots and water to boil in a heavy-bottomed saucepan. Lower heat and simmer, covered, about 30 minutes, stirring occasionally.
2. Puree in food mill or processor until smooth. Mix in sugar, salt and horseradish to taste. Serve warm or chilled.

Serves 6-8

MUSTARD FRUIT

Here's a simple condiment that can be prepared quickly and used with ham, pork or poultry. The fruit retains its character while gaining a hot-sweet quality. Any mixture of Pacific Northwest tree fruits will do. We like a combination of Anjou pears, tart Granny Smith apples and apricots. Use any mustard you wish.

> 2 cups sugar
> 1 1/2 cups water
> 4 tablespoons prepared mustard
> 1/2 teaspoon ground cardamom, 1/4
>   teaspoon aniseed and 2 whole
>   cloves tied in cheesecloth
> 1 teaspoon red pepper flakes (optional)
> 2 apples, cored and cut in medium
>   chunks
> 4 apricots, pitted and quartered
> 2 pears, cored and cut in medium chunks

Combine all ingredients except fruit and simmer 5 minutes. Add apples and apricots and simmer 1 minute. Add pears and simmer 2 minutes more. Place in glass jars and refrigerate at least 4 days. Serve chilled.

Makes about 6 cups

ONION AND RICE PUDDING

We first tasted this dish as an accompaniment to roasted lamb (another exception to the rule that Walla Walla Sweet onions should only be served raw). It accompanies any other meat, poultry or fish equally as well.

> 8 cups chopped Walla Walla Sweet onions
> 4 tablespoons butter
> 1/2 cup rice, cooked
> 3/4 cup grated Swiss cheese
>   Salt and pepper
> 1/2 cup grated Parmesan

1. Sauté onions in butter over lowest heat until they give up their liquid and it evaporates, about 30 minutes.
2. Mix onions, cooked rice, Swiss cheese and salt and pepper to taste. Scrape into buttered shallow baking dish, sprinkle with Parmesan and cover tightly with foil. Bake at 400° F for 45 minutes. Remove foil and bake 15 minutes to brown.

Serves 6-8

LENTIL PILAF

Combining lentils with brown rice makes a dish of complete protein. Add pine nuts, raisins and seasonings and you have a medley of flavors to accompany meat, poultry or fish, or stand on its own as a main course.

    1/2 cup chopped onion
    1 tablespoon vegetable oil
    2 tablespoons butter
    1 cup raw brown rice
    2 tablespoons tomato paste
    1/2 teaspoon cinnamon
    3 cups chicken stock (see Notes on
        Ingredients, page xi)
    1/2 pound lentils, rinsed
        Salt
    1/2 cup raisins
    1/2 cup pine nuts

1. In heavy-bottomed pot, sauté onion in vegetable oil and butter over low heat until limp, 6-8 minutes. Add brown rice and stir-fry 2-3 minutes.
2. Stir tomato paste and cinnamon into chicken stock. Add to rice mixture, raise heat to medium-high, cover tightly and bring to boil. Turn heat to low and simmer 20 minutes. Add lentils, bring to boil, skim foam and simmer, covered, 30 minutes more. Salt to taste. Stir in raisins and pine nuts and serve.

Serves 4-6

LENTIL PUREE

One variety of lentils grown in the Palouse hills of eastern Washington and western Idaho is Red Chief, which is sold with its seed coat removed. It cooks into a lovely yellow puree.

East Indians prize lentils as an inexpensive form of protein. They call them *dal*, a word also found on Indian restaurant menus referring to lentil puree.

This variation on *dal* is a delicious and nutritious appetizer. Serve it with bread for dipping; pita or one of the Indian breads is best.

    1 cup red lentils, rinsed
    3 1/2 cups water
    1 tablespoon minced fresh ginger
    1/2 teaspoon turmeric
        Salt
    2 tablespoons vegetable oil
    3 tablespoons butter, softened
    1 tablespoon minced garlic
    1 tablespoon lemon juice
        Tabasco

1. Place lentils, water, ginger, turmeric and salt to taste in saucepan. Cover and bring to boil. Skim foam, turn heat to medium-low and simmer, covered, until very tender, 30-40 minutes.
2. Beat lentils to puree. Beat in vegetable oil, butter, garlic, lemon juice and Tabasco to taste. Serve hot.

Serves 4

FOUR-ONION RELISH

Ordinarily, Walla Walla Sweet onions lose their character when cooked. Here is an exception. The mildness of the onions blends beautifully with the other varieties to produce a condiment for any meat or poultry dish.

    2 leeks
    3 scallions
    2 large Walla Walla Sweet onions
    2 large red onions
    5 tablespoons unsalted butter
    1/2 teaspoon sugar
    2 tablespoons balsamic vinegar
    1 teaspoon minced fresh rosemary
        Salt and pepper

Cut leeks, scallions, Walla Walla Sweets and red onions into 1/4-inch dice. Stir-fry in butter over medium-high heat until liquid has evaporated, about 10 minutes. Sprinkle with sugar, vinegar, rosemary and salt and pepper to taste. Continue stir-frying until onions begin to brown at edges. Serve warm or at room temperature.

Serves 4-6

ROASTED SUMMER VEGETABLES

In this dish, similar to ratatouille, the vegetables take on a nutty flavor from the roasting. The texture also is firmer than that of the classic French preparation. Serve it with any meat or fish.

>   1 medium eggplant
>   Salt
>   1/3 cup olive oil, extra-virgin if possible
>   1 1/2 pounds tomatoes, peeled, cored and
>   sliced thinly
>   1 pound medium Russet potatoes, peeled
>   and cut in 8 wedges
>   1/2 pound medium Walla Walla Sweet
>   onions, cut in 6 wedges
>   1/2 pound zucchini, cut in 1-inch-thick
>   pieces
>   2 stalks celery, cut in 1-inch lengths
>   1/4 cup chopped parsley
>   3 tablespoons chopped fresh mint
>   3 tablespoons chopped fresh basil
>   2 tablespoons chopped fresh oregano
>   1 teaspoon minced garlic
>   Salt and pepper
>   2 pinches sugar

1. Cut eggplant into 1-inch chunks, salt thoroughly and allow to sweat while other vegetables are prepared. Wipe off salt and pat dry.
2. Line baking pan with heavy foil. Oil with 2 tablespoons of the olive oil. Spread half the tomato slices evenly over the foil.
3. Toss vegetables with remaining olive oil. Add herbs, garlic and salt and pepper to taste. Toss gently. Distribute mixture over tomato slices. Top with remaining tomato slices. Sprinkle with sugar. Roast 30 minutes at 400° F. Remove from oven and stir gently to redistribute vegetables. Roast 30-35 minutes more.

Serves 6-8

WILD RICE PILAF WITH WILD MUSHROOMS

Although wild rice is cultivated in the Pacific Northwest and wild mushrooms are widely available in markets, this recipe smacks of foraging, eating off the land. It has strong flavors and goes well with any meat. Serve it with game, a salad of "wild" greens dressed in an herb vinaigrette and a full-bodied Pacific Northwest Merlot, and you have a memorable meal.

>   1/2 pound wild mushrooms, cut in small
>   pieces
>   4 tablespoons butter
>   1 teaspoon minced fresh marjoram
>   2 tablespoons Madeira
>   2 small leeks, white part minced
>   5 1/2 cups meat stock (see Notes on
>   Ingredients, page xi)
>   1 pound wild rice, rinsed and drained
>   Salt and pepper

1. Sauté mushrooms in half the butter over medium-high heat until moisture has evaporated, stirring in marjoram after a few minutes. Add Madeira and, stirring, cook until it evaporates. Remove from heat and set aside.
2. In large saucepan, sauté leeks in remaining butter over medium heat until soft but not colored, about 10 minutes. Add meat stock and bring to boil. Add wild rice and lightly salt and pepper. Turn heat to medium-low, cover and simmer for about 40 minutes, until rice is tender but firm in the center.
3. Fifteen minutes before rice is cooked, stir in mushrooms. Correct seasoning.

Serves 6-8

SPOON BREAD WITH WILD MUSHROOMS

Spoon bread, an American classic, is here enhanced by wild mushrooms. Any type will do nicely. Serve this with roasted meat or poultry, perhaps on Thanksgiving, when time-honored American dishes are especially appropriate.

1 tablespoon minced shallots
3 tablespoons butter
*½ pound wild mushrooms, cut in
  small pieces*
1 teaspoon minced fresh thyme
2 cups milk
*⅔ cup cornmeal
  Salt and Pepper*
4 tablespoons butter
4 egg yolks, beaten lightly
4 tablespoons Parmesan
4 egg whites

1. Sauté shallots in the 3 tablespoons butter over medium-low heat until soft, about 3 minutes. Add mushrooms and thyme, raise heat to medium-high and sauté, stirring, until moisture has evaporated. Remove from heat.
2. Bring milk to boil in heavy saucepan. Whisk in cornmeal in a steady stream. Salt and pepper to taste. Beat in the 4 tablespoons butter a tablespoon at a time. Remove from heat and beat in egg yolks. Stir in Parmesan. Cool slightly and fold in mushrooms.
3. Whip egg whites until stiff but not dry. Fold into cornmeal mixture.
4. Scrape into buttered 2-quart shallow baking dish. Bake at 350° F for about 35 minutes, until puffy and brown.

Serves 6-8

CURRIED RICES WITH DRIED FRUITS

This savory, nutritious accompaniment to meat or fish is splendid in the winter, when local fresh fruits in the Pacific Northwest are limited to apples and pears. In addition to the apricots and currants called for here, other dried fruits may be included or substituted. Drying fruits at home has become increasingly popular, and many people's larders are well stocked for the cold months when orchards are bare.

1 cup dried apricots
1 cup dried black currants
*2 pounds long-grained white rice
  Chicken stock (see Notes on
  Ingredients, page xi)*
1 pound wild rice, rinsed and drained
1 medium onion, chopped finely
*1 large apple, peeled, cored and
  chopped finely*
*1 large pear, peeled, cored and
  chopped finely*
1 cup butter
1 tablespoon curry powder
*1 cup slivered almonds, toasted in a
  dry skillet*
*¼ cup chopped fresh cilantro
  Salt and pepper*

1. Soak apricots and currants in warm water for 30 minutes. Drain and chop finely.
2. Cook white rice according to package directions, substituting chicken stock for water.
3. Cook wild rice according to package directions. Combine cooked rices.
4. Meanwhile, sauté onion, apple and pear in butter until just soft, about 5 minutes. (If the pear is quite ripe, as it should be, add it to the skillet for only the final 2 minutes.) Stir in curry powder, dried fruits and almonds and sauté briefly until the butter and curry powder coat the mixture.
5. Toss rices and fruit mixture with cilantro to combine. Salt and pepper to taste. Scrape mixture into lightly buttered baking dish, cover with foil and bake at 375° F for 30 minutes.

Serves 6-8

OKANAGAN VALLEY

An Orchard-Dotted Shangri-La

"They call this Shangri-la, you know," Alice Polesello said, bending into a large wooden bin of McIntosh apples and scooping out an armful. "It is," she added, transferring the apples to a box as she spoke, "the nicest place in the world." Her husband, Jerry, grinned in affirmation. "They'll plant me here," he said.

The Polesellos were talking about the Okanagan Valley in south-central British Columbia. Formed during North America's last ice age, about 10,000 years ago, the valley cuts through a plateau between mountain ranges. Beginning near Armstrong, BC, it twists 100 miles south to the US border and then stretches another 60 miles to the Columbia River. North of the border, it's spelled with only one "o." South, the second "a" becomes a second "o." By any name, it smells as sweet when the fruit ripens in the orchards that it shelters from one end to the other.

Bordered by semiarid hills, some of which, particularly on the American side, are as raw as a cowpuncher's knuckles, the Okanagan contains precious water and offers a mild climate, with warm days and cool nights–perfect, once irrigation pipes are added, for growing tree fruits. This was not immediately apparent, and it was not until the late 19th century that orchards were established on a large scale. Before then, the valley was cattle country, with bunchgrass in the hills and water in the hollows. A lot of

DESSERTS

water, too. In Canada, in fact, the valley floor contains a series of elongated lakes. (The principal one, Okanagan, is home to North America's own Loch Ness monster, fetchingly called Ogopogo.) Near the border, the valley narrows, and the Okanagan River emerges, flowing south to join the mighty Columbia.

The Polesellos live in Summerland, near the southwestern shore of Okanagan Lake, where the climate, unlike farther north, is ideal not only for apples and pears but also for soft fruits like peaches and plums. They have 35 acres of orchards, a roadside enterprise called Blossom Fruit Stand, where the orchards' wealth is sold from late June to mid-October, four grown children and a life of hard work that they wouldn't exchange for a royal title. They explained this quickly, for customers thronged the fruit stand.

"A half hour, and I can be skiing," Jerry said, pointing west. "Fifteen minutes, and I can be fishing for trout," he said, pointing east, toward the lake. "Ten minutes, and I can be cross-country skiing," he said, pointing west again. "Half an hour, and I can be hunting moose and elk and whitetail deer."

"And then there's the weather," Alice said. "And all the fruits in the world," Jerry said. "It's unbelievable at blossom time."

"Paradise," Alice said.

"All the fruit in the world" is only a slight exaggeration. Jerry ticked off his orchards' bounty, in chronological order: "First come the cherries, sweet and sour. Then apricots, peaches, plums, prunes [also called prune plums], pears–Bartletts, Anjou and Flemish. And the apples–Macs [McIntosh], Spartans, Delish [Common, Red and Golden] and Newtons [also known as Newtown Pippins]." In other words, on their 35 acres, the Polesellos produce the full, glorious panoply of Pacific Northwest tree fruits, two of which, apples and pears, make the region famous from Dubai to Tokyo.

Alice offered a tour of the apple bins. "The Macs are ready first. They're a softer apple than many of the others, really good for both cooking and eating. The Spartans come next. They're a cross between a Mac and a Red Delish, with the flavor of the Mac and the keeping quality of the Red Delish. Then the Red Delicious, which comes from the Common Delicious, because people decided they wanted a redder apple. Personally, I like the flavor of the Common much, much better. The Red Delish is mainly for eating fresh. The Golden Delish, on the other hand, is great for cooking. Then the Newton, a hard, hard green apple that really isn't good for eating until it's mellowed in storage for two or three months. They're good to eat fresh– Jerry likes them best–and they cook well."

Besides tree fruits, the Okanagan Valley is widely known for two other gustatory products: honey and wine. The former is a by-product of the bees needed to pollinate the fruit crops. The latter is the result of a fairly recent discovery that wine grapes flourish on the valley's dry hillsides. A dozen wineries, all specializing in white varieties, now dot the valley, most of them established in the past decade. Some have taken over land where orchards once stood. The Polesellos are unperturbed. "There aren't nearly as many acres of orchards here as there once were," Jerry said. "A lot of land has been taken for housing. Some is going back to horses and so on, like it used to be. People like their five acres of pasture and their horses, eh? With the dwarf [tree] varieties being planted now, though, we can still produce as much as before, even with less acres. There's one thing you don't have to worry about, though. As long as this valley exists, there'll be fruit trees here. They say it's the best in the world."

The Okanagan Valley, spanning the border of eastern Washingon and British Columbia (see overleaf), is one of the northernmost orchard regions on the continent. Its harvests provide the ingredients for such outstanding dishes as apfelsahnetorte, while berries grown in other parts of the Pacific Northwest can end up in concoctions such as this chocolate paté with raspberry sauce and Chantilly cream (recipe on page 112).

DESSERTS

Hazelnut Pie
with Brandy
Cream

Hazelnut
Soufflé with
Hazelnut
Sauce

HAZELNUT PIE WITH BRANDY CREAM

Oregonians have long called hazelnuts by their botanical name, "filberts." In response to marketing imperatives, growers are trying to change that. Marketing is important, because Oregon produces nearly all the hazelnuts grown in the United States, up to 25,000 tons annually. That doesn't compare with the output of the world's largest producer, Turkey, but Oregon hazelnuts generally are larger and tastier and thus have earned their niche on the basis of quality.

This is a Pacific Northwest version of the South's pecan pie.

Pastry

1 1/2 cups ground toasted hazelnuts (see
    Notes on Ingredients, page xi)
1/2 cup powdered sugar
4 tablespoons butter, softened
2/3 cup flour
1 egg yolk

1. Combine ground hazelnuts and powdered sugar. Cream butter until light and fluffy. Beat in nut mixture and flour. Add egg yolk and beat until dough begins to form a ball (about 2 minutes in an electric mixer).
2. Press pastry into a 9-inch tart pan with removable bottom. Trim excess from around edges of pan. Cover with plastic wrap and refrigerate 1 hour.

Filling

4 tablespoons butter, softened
1 cup firmly packed dark brown sugar
2/3 cup light corn syrup
3 eggs
2 tablespoons brandy
1 teaspoon vanilla
    Pinch salt
1 cup toasted whole hazelnuts

1. Cream butter, brown sugar and corn syrup until smooth (about 2 minutes in electric mixer). Beat in eggs one at a time. Beat in brandy, vanilla and salt.
2. Pour filling into pastry shell. Sprinkle hazelnuts on top. Bake in bottom third of a 375°F oven for 40 to 50 minutes, until knife inserted in center comes out clean. Serve with Brandy Cream.

Serves 6-8

Brandy Cream

1 cup heavy cream
2 teaspoons super-fine sugar
2 tablespoons brandy

Combine ingredients and whip until cream forms soft peaks.

HAZELNUT SOUFFLÉ WITH HAZELNUT SAUCE

Some critics, arguing that there is no such thing as "Northwest Cuisine," also scoff at the dishes containing hazelnuts that would appear to qualify as part of that cuisine. We agree that "Northwest Cuisine" is too grand a term for the new cooking taking place in the Pacific Northwest. But those who sneer at hazelnuts deprive themselves, as this ultra-hazelnutty recipe demonstrates.

1 cup half-and-half
1 teaspoon vanilla
4 egg yolks, at room temperature
3 tablespoons sugar
1/4 cup flour
3/4 cup ground toasted hazelnuts (see
    Notes on Ingredients, page xi)
3 tablespoons butter, softened
3 tablespoons Frangelico liqueur
6 egg whites
    Hazelnut Sauce (recipe follows)

1. Bring half-and-half and vanilla to a boil. Remove from heat. Whisk in egg yolks and sugar until mixture is creamy. Whisk in flour until smooth. Return to

medium-low heat and stir until mixture becomes very thick. Remove from heat.

2. Stir in hazelnuts, butter and Frangelico. Cool until mixture is barely warm.
3. Generously butter a 3-inch-deep by 11-inch-long oval glass dish. Sprinkle insides generously with sugar.
4. Whip egg whites until stiff but not dry. Fold one-quarter of whites into cooled custard until mixture is lightened. Gently fold in remaining whites, but do not overmix.
5. Pour mixture into oval dish. Bake at 375°F for 20-25 minutes, until soufflé is browned on top and fairly firm to the touch. Serve warm with Hazelnut Sauce.

Serves 6-8

Hazelnut Sauce

2 cups milk
¹/₂ cup sugar
6 egg yolks
¹/₂ cup ground toasted hazelnuts
1 tablespoon Frangelico liqueur

Bring milk and sugar to boil. Turn heat down to simmer. Whisk together egg yolks, ground hazelnuts and Frangelico. Gradually whisk nut mixture into hot milk until mixture becomes thick and smooth. Serve warm.

HAZELNUT TORTE WITH BLUEBERRY SAUCE

Northern Italians usually make this light cake with almonds. Hazelnuts are a perfect substitute, however. Be sure to grind them, or grate them finely, to achieve the proper texture. A food processor will not produce a fine-enough flour.

3 tablespoons white bread crumbs
³/₄ cup rye bread crumbs
³/₄ cup whole-wheat bread crumbs
¹/₄ cup rum
4 eggs
1 cup sugar
1¹/₂ cups ground toasted hazelnuts (see Notes on Ingredients, page xi)
1 teaspoon lemon zest
¹/₄ teaspoon cinnamon
¹/₈ teaspoon ground cloves
Blueberry Sauce (recipe follows)

1. Fit circle of greased waxed paper into a 9-inch springform pan. Butter sides of pan and sprinkle with the white bread crumbs.
2. Combine rye and whole-wheat crumbs with rum and set aside.
3. Separate 2 of the eggs. Beat the 2 whole eggs and the 2 yolks with the sugar until thick and lemon-colored. Beat in crumb-rum mixture, hazelnuts, lemon zest, cinnamon and cloves.
4. Whip the 2 egg whites until stiff but not dry. Fold into batter.
5. Pour into springform pan. Bake at 350°F for about 30 minutes, until knife inserted in center comes out dry. Remove sides of pan and let cake cool. Serve slightly warm or at room temperature with Blueberry Sauce.

Serves 6-8

Blueberry Sauce

1 pint blueberries
1 tablespoon sugar (or to taste)
1 teaspoon lemon juice

Combine blueberries and sugar. Puree in blender, food mill or processor. Stir in lemon juice.

Amaretti-
Blackberry
Tart

Poached
Peaches with
Blackberry
Sauce and
Zabaione
Cream

AMARETTI-BLACKBERRY TART

Our friend Sammy Knox of Bremerton, Washington, serves this beautiful, flavorful tart at her Cafe Sheridan. So popular is it that she freezes plenty of blackberries in the autumn so her customers aren't disappointed in the winter.

Amaretti, Italian macaroons, are widely available in this country and are even being made domestically. No other cookie can quite substitute in this recipe.

9-inch tart shell (see below)
1/2 cup crushed amaretti
2 cups blackberries
3 eggs
1 cup sugar
1 teaspoon vanilla
10 tablespoons unsalted butter
1/3 cup flour

1. Fill tart shell with crushed amaretti. Layer blackberries on top. Refrigerate while proceeding.
2. Beat eggs, sugar and vanilla until thick and lemon-colored.
3. Melt butter in saucepan until golden brown. (Be careful not to burn.) Remove from heat and mix in flour. Beat into egg mixture.
4. Pour batter over blackberries in tart shell. Bake at 350°F for 50-55 minutes. Cool to room temperature before removing from pan. Serve with lightly sweetened, lightly whipped cream.

Serves 6-8

Tart Shell

1 cup flour
1 tablespoon sugar
6 tablespoons unsalted butter, softened
1 egg yolk
1 tablespoon water

1. Mix flour and sugar. Work butter into mixture with pastry blender or fingers until it resembles coarse meal. Beat egg yolk with water and work into mixture until dough holds together. Wrap in plastic wrap and refrigerate for 1 hour.
2. Roll out dough on lightly floured surface to a round slightly larger than tart pan. Line 9-inch tart pan with removable bottom with dough. Trim off excess around edges.

POACHED PEACHES WITH BLACKBERRY SAUCE AND ZABAIONE CREAM

Blackberries, wild and cultivated, cover the Pacific Northwest, especially on the wet, or west, side of the mountain ranges. Cultivated hybrids have many names: Logan, Boysen, Marion, to name a few. Wild blackberries crowd backcountry roadsides.

Peach production in the Pacific Northwest pales in comparison to that of berries. Nonetheless, when local peaches come on the market, they're greeted enthusiastically by knowledgeable cooks. Combining them with Blackberry Sauce results in a memorable late-summer dessert.

1 1/2 cups sugar
3 cups water
3 peaches
Blackberry Sauce (recipe follows)
Zabaione Cream (recipe follows)

1. Combine sugar and water and bring to boil, stirring to dissolve sugar. Simmer 5 minutes.
2. Raise heat slightly, add peaches and simmer 10 minutes, or until tender. Remove with slotted spoon and cool. Cool syrup.
3. Peel cooled peaches, halve and remove pits. (Peaches can be kept, in the syrup, in the refrigerator until ready to serve. Drain peaches before proceeding.)
4. Divide Blackberry Sauce among dessert plates. Place peach half, cut side down, in center of each plate. Spoon Zabaione Cream on and around peaches. Garnish with whole blackberries.

Serves 6

Blackberry Sauce

1 pint blackberries
1 tablespoon sugar (or to taste)
1 teaspoon lemon juice

Combine blackberries and sugar and let stand 10 minutes to dissolve sugar and release berry juices. Puree in blender, food mill or processor. Strain, if desired, to remove seeds. Stir in lemon juice.

Zabaione Cream

6 egg yolks
$1/2$ cup sugar
$2/3$ cup orange-flavored liqueur
1 cup heavy cream
2 tablespoons sugar
3 tablespoons orange-flavored liqueur

1. Bring water to boil in bottom of double boiler, making certain top part does not touch water.
2. Whip egg yolks with the $1/2$ cup sugar until sugar is entirely dissolved and the mixture becomes fluffy and light-colored. Slowly stir in $2/3$ cup liqueur. Transfer mixture to top of double boiler.
3. Whisk constantly until mixture thickens enough to hold its shape in a spoon, about 5 minutes. Do not allow mixture to boil. Remove from heat and whisk 2-3 minutes to cool. Lay round of lightly buttered waxed paper on mixture and refrigerate 1 hour.
4. Whip cream with 2 tablespoons sugar. Stir in 3 tablespoons liqueur. Combine with chilled zabaione.

PEARS ON PASTRY WITH OREGON BLUE CHEESE AND BLUEBERRY COULIS

Unless you use frozen puff pastry, this dessert is time-consuming. With frozen pastry, on the other hand, it's a snap. If you choose to make your own pastry, consult a good French cookbook. Use one of the better cooking pears: Bosc, Comice or Bartlett.

6 ounces $1/4$-inch-thick puff pastry dough
3 pears, peeled and cored
3 tablespoons butter
3 tablespoons sugar
1 cup cassis liqueur
1 ounce Oregon Blue cheese, at room temperature
2 ounces cream cheese, at room temperature
$1/2$ cup coarsely chopped toasted hazelnuts (see Notes on Ingredients, page xi)
Blueberry Coulis (recipe follows)

1. Cut puff pastry into 6 2-by-4-inch rectangles. Arrange on a baking sheet and bake in the lower third of a 375°F oven for about 20 minutes, until golden brown. Cool. Reduce oven heat to 350°F.
2. Slice pears about $1/4$ inch thick. Sauté in butter and sugar until tender.
3. Boil cassis until reduced to $1/2$ cup.
4. Blend blue and cream cheeses. Spread on puff-pastry rectangles. Top with pear slices. Drizzle cassis on pears. Sprinkle with chopped hazelnuts.
5. Warm through in oven, about 1 minute.
6. Spoon Blueberry Coulis over pears and serve warm.

Serves 6

Blueberry Coulis

1 pint blueberries
1 tablespoon sugar
1 tablespoon butter
1 tablespoon cassis liqueur

Sauté blueberries and sugar in butter over medium heat, shaking the pan frequently, until berries begin to burst. Mash coarsely with fork. Cool until warm, not hot. Stir in cassis and serve.

Key Lime
Soufflé with
Raspberry
Sauce

Gratin of
Raspberries
with Ice
Cream

KEY LIME SOUFFLÉ WITH RASPBERRY SAUCE

Key Lime juice, with its unique tart-sweetness, is now widely available in bottles. However, lemon or regular lime juice can be substituted. Raspberry Sauce is an ideal accompaniment to this uncooked soufflé, but offer it sparingly since the raspberry flavor can overpower the other flavors.

> 2 tablespoons unflavored gelatin
> ¹/₂ cup cold water
> 6 eggs, separated
> 2 cups super-fine sugar
> ²/₃ cup Key Lime juice
> 3 cups heavy cream
>   Raspberry Sauce (recipe follows)

1. Soften gelatin in cold water. Dissolve by placing container of gelatin into pan of simmering water.
2. Beat egg yolks with sugar until thick and lemon-colored and no granules of sugar remain. Beat in Key Lime juice.
3. Whip egg whites until stiff but not dry. Whip cream.
4. Stir dissolved gelatin into lime mixture. Fold in egg whites and whipped cream. Beat briefly to combine well. Scoop into serving dish and refrigerate several hours until firm. Serve with Raspberry Sauce.

Serves 6-8

Raspberry Sauce

> 1 pint raspberries
> 1 tablespoon sugar (or to taste)
> 1 teaspoon lemon juice

Combine raspberries and sugar and let stand 10 minutes to dissolve sugar and release berry juices. Puree in blender, food mill or processor. Strain, if desired, to remove seeds. Stir in lemon juice.

Note: *Any type of berries will make an excellent sauce for the soufflé. Frozen berries, defrosted, are fine, too, but added sugar might not be necessary.*

GRATIN OF RASPBERRIES WITH ICE CREAM

Raspberries, red and black, are big business in the Pacific Northwest. Black raspberries are often confused with blackberries, but a simple test differentiates them: a raspberry pulls away from its core, or "receptacle," when picked; a blackberry's core is part of the fruit.

While the choice here is raspberries, red or black, blackberries would be perfectly acceptable for this quick and dramatic dessert. The liqueur called for is based on Loganberries from Whidbey Island in Puget Sound. Any berry-flavored liqueur may be substituted.

> 6 egg yolks
> 3 tablespoons sugar
> 1¹/₂ teaspoons orange zest
> 2 tablespoons Whidbeys Liqueur
> 1 cup whipping cream
> 3 cups raspberries
>   Vanilla ice cream

1. Bring water to boil in bottom of double boiler, making certain top part does not touch water.
2. Whip egg yolks with sugar and orange zest until sugar is entirely dissolved and the mixture becomes fluffy and light-colored. Slowly stir in liqueur. Transfer mixture to top of double boiler.
3. Whisk constantly until mixture thickens enough to hold its shape in a spoon, about 5 minutes. Do not allow mixture to boil. Remove from heat and whisk 2-3 minutes to cool. Lay round of lightly buttered waxed paper on mixture and refrigerate 1 hour.
4. Whip cream until thick. Combine with chilled egg mixture.
5. Divide berries among 6 gratin dishes. Top each with scoop of ice cream. Spoon cream mixture over ice cream. Place about 2 inches below preheated broiler. Broil until cream mixture becomes puffy and browned, about 2 minutes. Serve immediately.

Serves 6

RASPBERRY CAKE

Nearly all of Canada's commercial red raspberry crop is grown in the Fraser River Valley around Clearbrook, British Columbia. The soil, rainfall and climate–mild winters, warm summers–are ideal, and raspberry plantings have increased enormously in recent years.

Naturally, residents of the valley have become accustomed to an ample supply of red raspberries, and home cooks have developed many recipes for their use. Here, for example, is a cake developed by Alice Willms of Clearbrook.

> 1/3 cup butter, softened
> 1 cup sugar
> 1 egg
> 1 teaspoon vanilla
> 1 cup milk
> 2 cups flour
> 1 tablespoon baking powder
> 1/4 teaspoon salt
> 2 cups red raspberries
> Vanilla Icing (recipe follows)

1. Cream butter and sugar until smooth (about 2 minutes in electric mixer). Beat in egg, vanilla and milk.
2. Mix flour, baking powder and salt. Stir dry ingredients into egg-milk mixture until well blended, but do not overmix. Pour batter into buttered and floured baking pan. Scatter raspberries evenly on top. Bake at 375°F for 30-40 minutes, until a knife inserted in center comes out dry.
3. Frost with Vanilla Icing while cake is still slightly warm.

Serves 6-8

Vanilla Icing

> 2 cups powdered sugar, sifted
> 1/4 cup butter, softened
> 1/4 teaspoon salt
> 1 teaspoon vanilla
> 3-4 tablespoons milk

Beat sugar and butter until creamy, then beat in other ingredients. Add more sugar if icing is too thin, or more milk if it's too thick.

BERRY COMPOTE

From June until late autumn, the Pacific Northwest abounds with berries. This recipe is meant to suggest one method of enjoying them. Since their seasons overlap, try a compote of strawberries and raspberries. Or try raspberries and blueberries. Or add some blackberries. The point is, every combination yields its own flavor.

A berry compote can be an end unto itself (with a bit of cream or slightly whipped cream), or a topping for ice cream or pound cake.

> 1/2 cup kirsch
> 1/2 cup sugar
> 5 cups berries, any combination
> 6 tablespoons butter, softened

1. Combine kirsch and sugar in a large skillet. Simmer gently over medium heat to form a light syrup and burn off the alcohol.
2. Add berries and cook 3-4 minutes, shaking pan to coat berries with syrup. Add butter and cook, still shaking pan, until butter has melted. Stir gently so as not to break up berries. Serve warm.

Serves 6-8

Note: *If using large strawberries, slice them in half.*

**Chocolate
Paté with
Raspberry
Sauce and
Chantilly
Cream**

CHOCOLATE PATÉ WITH RASPBERRY SAUCE AND CHANTILLY CREAM

Because the paté freezes well (as does the Raspberry Sauce), it's ideal for holding against the day when unexpected guests arrive and something out of the ordinary is called for. Pluck it from the freezer, unmold according to the directions below, let it sit for an hour at room temperature (along with the Raspberry Sauce), whip up the Chantilly Cream and you have a quick dessert worthy of royalty.

Speaking of freezing, it's a good idea during raspberry season to make up a number of small containers of the Raspberry Sauce and freeze them for the winter. The simple puree can enliven many desserts.

> 1/2 pound semisweet chocolate, chopped
>   coarsely
> 4 tablespoons brandy
> 1/2 pound butter, softened
> 2 tablespoons super-fine sugar
> 3 eggs, separated
> 1 1/2 cups grated, toasted hazelnuts (see
>   Notes on Ingredients, page xi)
>   Raspberry Sauce (recipe follows)
>   Chantilly Cream (recipe follows)

1. Melt chocolate in pan set over simmering water. Remove from heat, add brandy and stir. Cool to room temperature.
2. Cream butter and sugar until fluffy. (Do this with an electric beater, as a food processor will heat the mixture too much.) Beat egg yolks one at a time by hand into butter mixture. Beat in hazelnuts and cooled chocolate.
3. Whip egg whites until soft peaks form. Fold into chocolate mixture one-quarter at a time just until no traces of the whites are visible.
4. Brush inside of 1 1/2 -quart loaf pan with vegetable oil, inverting pan on paper towel to allow excess oil to run out. Scrape batter into loaf pan and refrigerate overnight.
5. To unmold, run sharp knife around inside of pan. Dip bottom of pan in hot water for 15 seconds. Place platter upside down on pan and invert. Rap on counter and paté should unmold. If not, repeat entire unmolding process. Smooth sides of paté with spatula.
6. To serve, slice paté to desired thickness. Place slices on cold dessert plates. Spoon Raspberry Sauce over half of each slice, allowing sauce to run onto plate. Top with ribbon of Chantilly Cream and garnish with sprig of mint.

Serves 6-8

Raspberry Sauce

> 1 pint raspberries
> 1 tablespoon sugar (or to taste)
> 1 teaspoon lemon juice

Combine raspberries and sugar and let stand 10 minutes to dissolve sugar and release berry juices. Puree in blender, food mill or processor. Pass through food mill to remove seeds. Stir in lemon juice.

Chantilly Cream

> 1 cup whipping cream
> 2 teaspoons super-fine sugar
> 1/2 teaspoon vanilla

Combine ingredients and whip until cream forms soft peaks.

BROILED STRAWBERRY GALETTE

While there's nothing humdrum about a traditional strawberry tart, this preparation is startlingly different. Try it in midsummer, with local berries that are similar in size and ripe clear through. The big berries that are available out of season have little juice and less flavor.

> ³/₄ cup butter, softened
> 1³/₄ cups flour, sifted
> ¹/₂ cup powdered sugar
> 4 egg yolks
> ¹/₂ teaspoon vanilla
> 3 tablespoons red currant jelly
> 1 quart strawberries, hulled
> 1 cup crème fraîche (see Notes on
>   Ingredients, page xi)
> 1 cup Zabaione Cream (recipe follows)
> 1 cup firmly packed dark brown sugar

1. With pastry blender or fingers, blend butter into flour, then add powdered sugar, egg yolks and vanilla and blend until mixture has coarse-crumb texture. Press into ball and knead on lightly floured surface until smooth. Wrap in plastic wrap and refrigerate 30 minutes, until firm.
2. Roll out dough to 10-inch circle. Place on baking sheet and flute edges between fingers and thumb. Chill 30 minutes.
3. Pierce dough all over with fork. Bake at 350°F for 15-20 minutes, until lightly browned.
4. Melt red currant jelly in small pan over low heat and brush on pastry shell.
5. Leaving a 1-inch border, arrange berries in concentric circles on pastry shell.
6. Whisk crème fraîche until smooth. Fold in Zabaione Cream. Spoon mixture over berries. Sprinkle evenly with brown sugar.
7. Place about 4 inches below preheated broiler. Watching carefully, broil until brown sugar begins to bubble and lightly caramelize. Serve warm.

Serves 6-8

Zabaione Cream

> 3 egg yolks
> ¹/₄ cup sugar
> ¹/₃ cup orange-flavored liqueur
> ¹/₂ cup whipping cream
> 1 tablespoon sugar
> 1¹/₂ tablespoons orange-flavored liqueur

1. Bring water to boil in bottom of double boiler, making certain top part does not touch water.
2. Whip egg yolks with the ¹/₄ cup sugar until sugar is entirely dissolved and the mixture becomes fluffy and light-colored. Slowly stir in ¹/₃ cup liqueur. Transfer mixture to top of double boiler.
3. Whisk constantly until mixture thickens enough to hold its shape in a spoon, about 5 minutes. Do not allow mixture to boil. Remove from heat and whisk 2-3 minutes to cool. Lay round of lightly buttered waxed paper on mixture and refrigerate 1 hour.
4. Whip cream with 1 tablespoon sugar. Stir in 1¹/₂ tablespoons liqueur. Combine with chilled zabaione.

CHERRY FRITTERS WITH TWO SAUCES

Dessert fritters need no more adornment than a dusting of powdered sugar. Serving them with two sauces, however, elevates a homely standby to an elegant dessert. Cherries are the fruit of choice here, but any stone fruit–or combination of them–will produce tasty fritters.

> 1½ cups chopped sweet cherries
> 3 tablespoons kirsch
> 2 eggs separated
> 1 tablespoon butter, softened
> ⅔ cup flat beer
> ¼ teaspoon salt
> 1 tablespoon sugar
> 1 cup flour
>   Vegetable oil for frying
>   Cherry Caramel Sauce
>   (recipe follows)
>   Sour Cream Sauce (recipe follows)

1. Soak fruit in kirsch and set aside.
2. Beat egg yolks, butter and beer until thick. Mix in dry ingredients.
3. Whip egg whites until stiff but not dry. Fold into batter. Refrigerate for about 2 hours.
4. Drain fruit and fold into batter.
5. Heat about 2 inches of vegetable oil in heavy skillet until a haze forms (360°F). Drop batter into oil a tablespoonful at a time. Fry until golden brown. Remove with slotted spoon and drain on paper towels. Serve warm with Cherry Caramel Sauce and Sour Cream Sauce for dipping.

Serves 4-6

Cherry Caramel Sauce

> ½ pound sweet cherries, chopped
> 2-3 tablespoons water
> ½ cup sugar
> 1 teaspoon corn syrup
> 1 tablespoon kirsch

1. Simmer cherries in water until soft. Puree in food mill or processor.
2. Moisten sugar with several tablespoons water in heavy saucepan. Add corn syrup. Cook over medium heat to dissolve sugar. Raise heat to high and boil until mixture turns a deep amber, but not dark brown. Remove from heat.
3. Stir in cherry puree and strain. Stir in kirsch. Cool to room temperature.

Sour Cream Sauce

> ½ cup heavy cream
> ¼ cup sour cream
> 4 teaspoons sugar
> 1 teaspoon kirsch

Combine ingredients and beat until smooth.

BOYSENBERRY CURD TARTLETS

Boysenberries, the largest of the commercially significant blackberry hybrids in the Pacific Northwest, are noted for their complex flavor, favorable sugar-acid balance and juiciness. Here, they are transformed into a royally colored dessert. This recipe was developed by Angela Owens, daughter of Angelo and Virginia Pellegrini (see page 41), friend of the authors and a renowned cook in Seattle and Olympia, Washington.

> 1 pint Boysenberries
> 1 tablespoon lemon juice
> ½ cup sugar
> 6 tablespoons butter
> 2 eggs
> 3 egg yolks
>   Cream Cheese Pastry (recipe
>   follows)

1. Puree berries with lemon juice in blender, food mill or processor. Combine with sugar (adjust amount according to taste and tartness of berries) and butter in top of a double boiler. Place over barely simmering, not boiling,

water, taking care that the top does not touch the water. Cook just until sugar and butter have melted and mixture is warm, not hot.

2. Remove from heat. Lightly beat together eggs and egg yolks. Stir into berry mixture, return to heat and cook, stirring, until mixture thickens, about 20 minutes. Remove from heat and chill. Spoon chilled curd into tartlet shells and serve.

Serves 8-10

Cream Cheese Pastry

3 ounces cream cheese, softened
8 tablespoons butter, softened
1 cup flour

Beat cream cheese and butter to combine. Blend mixture into flour by hand, kneading lightly. Press dough into tartlet pans. (Any size will do. Or a 9-inch tart pan may be substituted.) Weight down pastry with pie weights or dried beans and bake at 400° F for about 15 minutes, until lightly browned. Cool slightly before removing weights or beans. Cool completely before filling with curd.

TUXEDO PIE

Lynda Nestelle, a "food engineer" in Portland, Oregon, develops recipes for clients all over the country. In her spare time she enjoys experimenting with local ingredients. This recipe, for example, resulted from her love of Willamette Valley Marionberries, currently the favorite hybrid blackberry in the valley. As its name implies, the pie has a formal appearance: black filling, glossy white meringue.

Don't be dismayed by the large amount of cornstarch called for. Marionberries are quite acid, and the acid breaks down the cornstarch's thickening capacity. If you're using a less acid berry, such as Evergreen blackberries, reduce the cornstarch to ¹/₂ cup.

3¹/₂ cups Marionberry juice (see note)
1¹/₂ cups sugar
³/₄ cup cornstarch
¹/₄ teaspoon cinnamon
4 egg yolks, beaten
¹/₃ cup lemon juice
3 tablespoons clarified butter (see note)
¹/₄ teaspoon salt
*   9-inch pie shell, baked until light brown*
4 egg whites
¹/₄ teaspoon cream of tartar
¹/₄ teaspoon vanilla
*   Dash nutmeg*
7 tablespoons sugar

1. Bring berry juice, 1¹/₂ cups sugar, cornstarch and cinnamon to boil over medium heat, stirring. Remove from heat. Stir 2-3 tablespoons of the hot liquid into the beaten egg yolks, then stir the yolks into the berry mixture. Turn heat to medium-low, and return saucepan to heat. Stir in lemon juice, clarified butter and salt. Cook at gentle simmer until mixture is just thickened. Pour into pie shell and set aside.

2. Whip egg whites with cream of tartar, vanilla, nutmeg and 7 tablespoons sugar. Whip until whites lose their shine and are quite stiff and dry. Spread meringue over warm filling, making certain meringue meets the crust all around to seal.

3. Bake at 400° F until light brown on top, about 10 minutes. Set aside in draft-free area to cool before serving.

Serves 6-8

Notes: *To make 3¹/₂ cups berry juice, crush 7-8 cups berries and strain.*
To clarify, melt 4 tablespoons of butter over very low heat in small saucepan. Carefully pour off melted butter, leaving milk solids behind. Clarifying the butter prevents the pie filling from being cloudy.

JERILYN'S BLACKBERRY COBBLER

Jerilyn Brusseau of Edmonds, Washington, has earned a national reputation for her fruit cobblers. Mainstays at her restaurant-bakery, brusseau's, the cobblers have moist tops and fillings of seasonal fruits. In all her cooking, Brusseau champions fresh local ingredients. Here she exploits the Pacific Northwest's magnificent blackberries. For this cobbler, she prefers the hybrid known as Marionberry because of its complex flavor and balance between sweet and acid. Any berry variety will do, however, and each produces its own distinctive flavor.

After they're picked, raspberries and blackberries tend to absorb and break up in water. Generally they don't need washing, but if they do, place them gently in a sink full of water and then quickly and carefully remove them.

Filling

6 cups blackberries
1¼ cups sugar (or to taste)
⅓ cup cornstarch

1. Sprinkle berries with 1 cup of the sugar and let stand 1 hour at room temperature. Drain, reserving juice.
2. Combine remaining sugar with cornstarch and reserved berry juice. Cook, stirring, over medium heat until mixture is thick, about 4 minutes. Cool slightly and pour over berries. Spoon berries into a 9-inch baking dish.

Topping

2 cups flour
1 cup sugar
1 tablespoon baking powder
1 teaspoon salt
1 cup milk
½ cup butter, melted
¼ teaspoon nutmeg
1 tablespoon sugar

1. Mix flour, 1 cup sugar, baking powder and salt. Beat in milk and butter just until batter is smooth, but don't over-mix.
2. Spoon batter over berries, carefully spreading to edges of dish to prevent excess juice from bubbling over during baking. Sprinkle with nutmeg and the remaining tablespoon of sugar.
3. Bake at 350° F for 35-40 minutes, until topping is golden brown. Cool slightly before serving. Serve with ice cream or heavy cream.

Serves 10-12

POTATO CUSTARD PIE

At a potato-recipe contest we helped judge in the central Washington town of Quincy, this recipe was the unanimous choice in the dessert category. Developed by Rhonda Rosenberger of Quincy, the pie has a golden color, a mashed-potato texture and a flavor hard to identify as coming from potatoes. Although Rosenberger owns and cooks at The Spud Shed Tavern and Deli in Quincy, this is a true farmhouse recipe.

2 tablespoons butter
¾ cup sugar
⅛ teaspoon salt
1 medium Russet potato, boiled and mashed
2 egg yolks, beaten
½ cup milk
2 tablespoons orange zest
2 tablespoons Grand Marnier
2 egg whites
9-inch pie shell

1. Beat butter, sugar and salt into mashed potato until mixture is creamy. Cool.
2. Beat egg yolks, milk, orange zest and Grand Marnier into cooled potato mixture. Whip egg whites until stiff but not dry. Fold into potato mixture. Scrape into pie shell. Bake at 375° F for 45 minutes. Serve warm or cool with topping of whipped cream flavored by Grand Marnier.

Serves 6-8

PEAR PANDOWDY

Bartlett pears retain their shape when cooked, and therefore are ideal for this down-home American classic. Serve it with lightly sweetened, lightly whipped cream.

6 pears, peeled, cored and sliced thinly
$^3/_4$ cup firmly packed brown sugar
$^1/_2$ teaspoon cinnamon
    Pinch nutmeg
$^1/_2$ teaspoon ground ginger
    Pinch salt
1$^1/_2$ cups flour
1$^1/_2$ tablespoons sugar
2$^1/_2$ tablespoons baking powder
$^1/_2$ teaspoon salt
6 tablespoons cold butter, cut into bits
2 tablespoons minced candied ginger
7-9 tablespoons milk

1. Toss pear slices with brown sugar, cinnamon, nutmeg, ground ginger and salt. Arrange evenly in buttered 9-inch-square baking dish or pan.
2. Sift together flour, sugar, baking powder and salt. With pastry blender or fingers, blend butter bits into flour mixture until mixture resembles coarse cornmeal. Stir in candied ginger. Sprinkle with 7 tablespoons of the milk and toss with a fork. Add more milk if necessary to make a soft dough.
3. Roll out dough to 1 inch larger than baking dish. Place over dish. Secure dough to edge of dish by dipping fork into milk and pressing dough around edge of dish. Trim off excess dough. Bake at 350°F for about 45 minutes, until crust is golden brown. Serve warm.
Serves 6-8

MARY MOORE'S OPEN-FACED PEAR PIE

Everyone in Oregon's Hood River Valley knows Mary Moore. For 30 years she was the driving force behind the smorgasbord at the grange hall in Pine Grove on Blossom Day. Widow of an orchardist, the octogenarian Moore knows the kitchen virtues of the valley's fruits as few do. Her most famous recipe, one the county agent annually serves on Horticulture Day to 400 guests, is this pie. For it, Moore prefers juicy Comice pears.

4 medium Comice pears, halved, peeled, cored and rubbed with lemon juice
    9-inch pie shell (recipe follows)
$^1/_4$ cup butter, softened
1 cup sugar
1 teaspoon vanilla
3 eggs
$^1/_8$ teaspoon salt
$^1/_4$ cup flour
$^1/_2$ teaspoon ground mace

1. Place pear halves cut side up in pie shell.
2. Cream butter, sugar and vanilla. Beat in eggs. Mix salt with flour and beat into egg mixture. Pour over pears, sprinkle with mace and bake at 350°F for 45 minutes. Serve warm or at room temperature.
Serves 6-8

Pie Shell

1 cup flour
$^1/_8$ teaspoon salt
$^1/_2$ cup shortening
1 egg, lightly beaten
$^1/_2$ teaspoon cider vinegar
    Water

Mix flour, salt and shortening with fingers until mixture resembles coarse cornmeal. Stir in egg. Mix vinegar with about $^1/_4$ cup water and add gradually while stirring until the dough forms a stiff ball. Roll out dough to fill pie pan and pat into place. Trim edges.

**Baked
Caramel
Pears**

**Bread
Pudding with
Apples and
Bourbon
Sauce**

BAKED CARAMEL PEARS

Bartletts or Comice are excellent pears for baking, but our favorite is the long-necked, russetted beauty called Bosc. Make sure the pears are thoroughly ripe. Any chopped nuts will do, but hazelnuts lend a Pacific Northwest touch. Corn syrup isn't essential to this dish, but its addition makes a softer caramel and prevents crystallization.

> 3 large pears, halved, cored and peeled
> ³/₄ cup sugar
> 1 tablespoon corn syrup
> 3 tablespoons unsalted butter, cut
>   into bits
> ¹/₂-²/₃ cup heavy cream
> 3 tablespoons chopped toasted hazelnuts
>   (see Notes on Ingredients,
>   page xi)

1. Place pears rounded side down in heavy flameproof dish (enameled iron is best). Sprinkle with sugar, drizzle with corn syrup and distribute butter bits evenly. Bake at 350°F for about 30 minutes, until pears are tender. Baste several times with juices from the dish.
2. Remove pears from dish, pouring juices from their cavities back into dish. Set dish on stove over high heat. Boil until mixture turns a deep amber—but not dark brown. Remove from heat and pour in cream slowly. (It will bubble and splatter, so take care.) Stir with a long-handled wooden spoon and return to heat, cooking and stirring until smooth.
3. Spoon caramel over pears on individual serving dishes, sprinkle with hazelnuts and serve warm.

Serves 6

BREAD PUDDING WITH APPLES AND BOURBON SAUCE

Pockets of commercial black-currant production are appearing again in the Pacific Northwest. For many years, it was illegal to grow black currants because they are host to a white-pine disease. Their return is good news, for these berries have a strong, wild flavor that is welcome in the kitchen. Because fresh black currants are still difficult to find, most cooks have to be content with dried. Here dried currants combine with apples to transform a standard American dessert into a Pacific Northwest special. One tradition not to be tampered with is the accompanying Bourbon Sauce.

> 1 cup dried black currants
> 5 eggs
> 4 egg yolks
> 1 cup sugar
>   Pinch salt
> 2 cups heavy cream
> 3 cups milk
> ¹/₂ teaspoon vanilla
> 16 small, thin slices stale French bread,
>   crusts removed
>   Softened butter
> 2 apples, peeled, cored and sliced thinly
>   Nutmeg
>   Powdered sugar
>   Bourbon Sauce (recipe follows)

1. Soak currants in warm water for 30 minutes.
2. Beat eggs, yolks, sugar and salt until well combined. Scald cream and milk in saucepan, then slowly beat into egg mixture. Stir in vanilla.
3. Generously butter bread slices on one side. Layer half the slices, butter side up, in a buttered 2-quart baking dish. Spread with the apple slices. Drain the currants and sprinkle them on the apples. Layer on the remaining bread slices, butter side up.
4. Pour custard through strainer into baking dish, taking care not to disarrange the bread slices. Sprinkle with nutmeg.
5. Place baking dish in larger pan and pour boiling water into larger pan to a depth of 1 inch. Bake at 375°F for about 45 minutes, until knife inserted in center comes out clean. Sprinkle with powdered sugar and serve warm with Bourbon Sauce.

Serves 6-8

Bourbon Sauce

    2 tablespoons sugar
    1 1/2 cups heavy cream
    1 1/2 teaspoons cornstarch dissolved in
        2 tablespoons water
    2 tablespoons bourbon
    1 tablespoon butter

Combine sugar and cream in small, heavy saucepan and cook over low heat, stirring often, until almost boiling. Remove from heat. Stir in cornstarch mixture until thickened. Stir in bourbon. Stir in butter bit by bit.

APFEL-SAHNETORTE

"It's a lot of work, but you end up with a wonderful cake that people like because it's not too sweet," says Irma Krauss of Kaleden, in British Columbia's Okanagan Valley, of this dessert. "Apple-whipped cream cake" in English, this is a German confection that Krauss, who came to the valley from Germany as a child, makes for special occasions. The apples come from her own orchard.

Cake

    2 eggs, separated
    2-3 tablespoons warm water
    1/2 cup sugar
    1 teaspoon vanilla
    1/2 cup flour
    1 teaspoon baking powder
    5 tablespoons cornstarch

1. Beat yolks with water. Add two-thirds of the sugar and the vanilla and beat until frothy and lemon-colored.
2. Whip egg whites with remaining sugar until stiff but not dry. Fold into yolk mixture. Combine dry ingredients and stir into wet mixture until just blended.
3. Fit a circle of greased and floured waxed paper into a greased and floured 9-inch springform pan. Pour in batter and bake at 350°F for about 20 minutes, until knife inserted in center comes out dry. Cool before filling.

Filling

    10-15 apples
    1/4-1/2 cup sugar
    2 tablespoons unflavored gelatin
    3 tablespoons cold water

1. Peel and core apples and cut into chunks. Cook over medium heat until very soft, sweetening with sugar to taste toward the end. Mash apples or put through food processor to make 4 cups applesauce. Cool.
2. Soften gelatin in cold water. Dissolve by placing container of gelatin into pan of simmering water. Stir into cooled applesauce and set aside to cool further.

Frosting

    1 cup sliced almonds
    1 tablespoon sugar
    2 tablespoons butter
    1 pint whipping cream
    2 tablespoons sugar
    1 tablespoon unflavored gelatin
    1 tablespoon cold water

1. Combine almonds, sugar and butter in frying pan over medium heat. Cook, stirring, until almonds turn golden. Set aside to cool.
2. Whip cream with sugar. Halfway through, add gelatin (softened in water, as above).

Assembly:

1. Remove cooled cake from pan and slice in half horizontally. Pile applesauce on bottom half, mounding slightly. Cover with top half of cake and pat down to evenly distribute applesauce.
2. Frost top and sides generously with whipped cream, reserving several tablespoonfuls.
3. Pat almonds around sides of cake. Decorate top with reserved whipped cream.
4. Chill in refrigerator overnight before serving.
Serves 6-10

APPLES IN PARCHMENT

Prepare parchment packets ahead of time (they don't need refrigeration), pop them into the oven while the main-course dishes are being cleared and you have a perfect dessert for a dinner party. Golden Delicious or, if you like more tartness, Granny Smith apples are excellent for cooking because they hold their shapes well under heat. Although no threat to the Red Delicious, Granny Smiths are steadily gaining popularity among Pacific Northwest growers. There's even a "blushing" variety that adds rouge to the Granny's familiar green cheeks.

> Unsalted butter, softened
> 6 tablespoons apricot jam
> 6 apples, peeled and cored
> 8 tablespoons coarsely chopped toasted
>   hazelnuts (see Notes on
>   Ingredients, page xi)
>   Cinnamon
>   Nutmeg
>   Dark rum

1. Cut out 6 15-inch squares of cooking parchment and lightly butter top side of each.
2. Spread 1 tablespoon of jam on half of each parchment square. Cut each apple into 6 slices and arrange in a star pattern atop the jam. Sprinkle apples with hazelnuts. Dot with butter and sprinkle with cinnamon and nutmeg. Splash about 1 tablespoon of the rum on each apple arrangement.
3. Prepare parchment packets in this way: Fold parchment over apples; to seal packet, take bottom corner of the folded side and fold up to create a triangle. Continue folding edge up and over every 2 inches as you work your way around packet; this forms a pleated border that seals the packet; at the final corner, turn the end under.
4. Place packets on baking sheet and bake at 375°F for 10-12 minutes, depending on firmness of apples. Open packets by cutting a cross in each with a sharp knife and folding parchment back. Serve hot.

Serves 6

APPLE SLICE

The residents of British Columbia's Okanagan Valley tend to be straightforward. Alice Polesello (featured at the beginning of this chapter) has no fancy name for this dessert. "Apple Slice" it is, then–a Polesello family favorite.

> 2 cups sifted flour
> 2 teaspoons baking powder
> $1/4$ teaspoon salt
> $1/2$ cup shortening
> $3/4$ cup sugar
> 1 egg
> 1 teaspoon vanilla
> 3-4 apples, peeled and cored
> $1/4$ cup brown sugar
> $1/4$ teaspoon nutmeg

1. Sift dry ingredients together.
2. Cream shortening. Beat in sugar. Beat in egg. Beat in vanilla. Add dry mixture and stir until just blended.
3. Pour half of batter into buttered 8-inch-square baking dish or pan. Smooth batter.
4. Slice apples very thinly, using vegetable peeler or grater. Spread slices on batter. Sprinkle with brown sugar and nutmeg. Pour on remaining batter and bake at 350°F for about 40 minutes, until knife inserted in center comes out dry. Sprinkle with sugar and serve with whipped cream or, as Alice does, ice cream.

Serves 6-8

MAIL-ORDER SOURCES
A sampling of vendors to aid in the search for Northwest ingredients.

Cheese

Blue Heron French Cheese Co.
2001 Blue Heron Drive
Tillamook, OR 97141
(503) 842-8281
Brie and Camembert

Pleasant Valley Dairy, Inc.
6804 Kickerville Road
Ferndale, WA 98248
(206) 366-5398
Farmhouse Gouda

Rogue River Valley Creamery
P.O. Box 3606
Central Point, OR 97502
(503) 664-2233
*Oregon Blue, cheddar, jack
and Colby cheeses*

Sally Jackson Cheese Co.
Star Route, Box 106
Oroville, WA 98844
(No phone)
Goat, sheep and cow cheeses and blends

Tillamook County Creamery Assoc.
P.O. Box 313
Tillamook, OR 97141
(503) 842-4481
Tillamook cheddar

Washington State
   University Creamery
Troy Hall 101
Pullman, WA 99164
(509) 335-7516
*Cougar Gold, cheddar and other
   cheeses aged in tins*

Fruits and Nuts

Cascade Harvest
Brewster, WA 98812
(509) 689-3201
Apples and pears

Harry & David
Bear Creek Orchards
Medford, OR 97501
(800) 547-3033
Apples and pears

Hazy Grove Nuts
P.O. Box 25753
Portland, OR 97225
(503) 244-0593
Hazelnuts

Pinnacle Orchards
P.O. Box 1068
Medford, OR 97501
(800) 547-0227
Apples, pears and hazelnuts

Serendipity Orchards
P.O. Box 303
Manson, WA 98831
(509) 687-3941
Red Delicious apples

Grains

St. Maries Wild Rice, Inc.
P.O. Box 293
St. Maries, ID 83861
(800) 225-9453
Wild rice

Seafood

Ekone Oyster Co.
Box 465
South Bend, WA 98586
(206) 875-5494
Smoked oysters

Hegg & Hegg
801 Marine Drive
Port Angeles, WA 98362
(206) 457-3344
*Smoked salmon, tuna, sturgeon, oysters,
   crab, clams and shrimp*

Imperial Salmon House, Ltd.
1632 Franklin Street
Vancouver, BC V5L 1P4
Canada
(604) 251-1114
Smoked salmon

Jet Set Sam
200 765 Powell St.
Vancouver, BC V6A 185
Canada
(604) 273-9917
*Prawns, shrimp, clams;
   airport to airport only*

Josephson's Smokehouse and Dock
P.O. Box 412
Astoria, OR 97103
(800) 772-3474
*Smoked salmon and fresh salmon, halibut,
   sturgeon, lingcod, tuna, shellfish, etc.*

The Lobster Man
1807 Mast Tower Road
Granville Island
Vancouver, BC V6H 3X7
Canada
(604) 687-4531
Live shellfish, including lobster

Port Chatham Packing Co.
632 NW 46th Street
Seattle, WA 98107
(206) 783-8200
Smoked salmon, sturgeon, trout and oysters

Pure Food Fish Market
1511 Pike Place Market
Seattle, WA 98101
(206) 622-5765
*Fresh salmon, Dungeness crab,
   oysters, geoduck, etc.*

Scimitar Meats
7352 SW Durham Road
Portland, OR 97224
(800) 553-9463
*Wine-cured smoked salmon, oysters,
   clams, shrimp (and meats)*

Specialty Seafoods
1719 13th Street
Anacortes, WA 98221
(206) 293-0611
Smoked salmon and oysters

Vegetables

Walla Walla Gardeners' Association
210 N. 11th Street
Walla Walla, WA 99362
(800) 553-5014
Walla Walla Sweet onions

INDEX